Praise f

When I met Joan forty years ago, I quickly realized she was a unique and special person with the ability to communicate and make a difference at a level beyond anything I had ever experienced. Joan's "Morning Messages" show that we, and the world, would be in a better place with a commitment to honest and effective communication.—Paul Zuelke, President, Zuelke and Associates

Joan's Morning Messages have brought great inspiration and encouragement to me and my staff. Always with great insight and wit, Joan brings wisdom in a unique way and provides a practical application to be used for every day!—Steven Hough, DDS, specialist in orthodontics

As a new orthodontist, I realized my patient exam presentation needed work, so I reached out to Joan. Her tempered encouragement, along with some helpful exercises, made a big difference. My exams now go much smoother and I am much more confident in the office and at home!—Dr. Joseph K. Ryan, DDS, MSD

Joan's messages have always made the connection between head and heart, with a goal of helping people make better connections with others. I learn something special and usable with each message and I always look forward to them with great delight!—Rev. Dan Holloway, author of *Knowing God More*

Joan's professional skill and commitment are extraordinary. Her messages are the best way ever to start the work week! I am so grateful for her coaching and inspiration.—Charles Wear, DDS, MS

"Monday Morning!" from Joan Garbo has been a staple to my team for many years. When I share her messages and quotes with my staff, I receive heart-felt replies indicating how much they have meant in a time of special need with a teammate or home!—Joseph Gray, DDS, MS

Joan Garbo's messages have been something I've looked forward to reading for many years. Each one has provided insights and guidance I use every day as a leader of my company.—Michael Zuelke, founder & CEO, ZuSo Technologies

Joan has made it her mission in life to bring value to the lives of anyone with whom she has contact. Throughout the decades I have known her, I cannot recall even a single time she has not brought a new light to my life and to my professional career. I am sure many lives have been touched with her words of wisdom, insights, and sense of humor. Mine certainly has, and I'm forever grateful.—Gib Snow, DDS, MS

Joan's "Morning Messages" serve as a call to action, reminding us of our need and duty to positively impact those around us. Reading them always makes me feel hopeful! A collection of business tips and inspirational stories all in one place—I can't wait to read Joan's new book.—Mary Kay Rosenberger, orthodontic consultant

Monday Morning Messages:
Kick-Start Your Week with the Power of Positivity

Joan Garbo

BAY CREEK PUBLISHING

MONDAY MORNING MESSAGES
October 2022

Photos on pp 42 and 50 are courtesy of Steven W. Hough.

Cover design by: Patrick Fisher
Interior design by: David K. Dodd

Library of Congress Control Number 2022946576
ISBN 978-0-9835670-7-3

Published by:
Bay Creek Publishing, LLC
PO Box 221697
St. Louis, MO 63122

Preface

In 2014, I began creating "Monday Morning Messages," short weekly essays for my clients as a way to support their morning *huddle* on the first day of the work week. The huddle is much like that used in sports—a brief meeting among the players to make up the game plan for the next move, and in an office the plan for the day. Designed to be read at the huddle, the purpose was to energize, inspire and create a focus on excellence in patient relations. Over the span of seven years, I went from weekly to bi-weekly and then monthly distribution to subscribers.

The essays in this book are based on several premises:

Life is a conversation—we must be conscientious in our speaking, especially in what we tell ourselves.

When we speak, we are creating the experience of our life. The basis of one's experience of life is 10% actual circumstances and 90% one's interpretation of those circumstances.

Integrity is the foundation of all relationships, whether those are personal, professional, or one's relationship to oneself.

Every business needs to train employees in the skills required of the job AND to train employees in how to provide an experience that turns the customers/clients/patients into "raving fans.

In my view, the key to service is creating an experience for your patient/client/customer that validates their decision to choose you as their provider. This can be achieved only when the employees, managers, and employers are aligned on the mission of the business and are committed to each other's success.

This is not a new concept and has been written about by brilliant authors in every business and profession. My intent in this book is to remind readers of the principles for success in life and how they can apply them on a frequent basis. While some people may wish to read this book from cover-to-cover, it is designed to be used as inspiration for "the moment" and is organized by topic of interest. Thus, the reader can choose an area of interest, flip to that chapter, and seek out the "message" for that day or week.

Finally, one of my foundational beliefs about life is that all of us can and do make a difference in life, and it is up to us to choose what that difference will be. Will we be a positive force for change or will we be "another brick on the load"? We cannot control the circumstances in life but we do have the ability to choose our interpretation and response to the challenges life presents. You may believe that only people with power and money can impact the direction of life, and on the macro level that may be true.

On the personal, micro level of life, though, we all have the power to alter the experience of life and bring joy and love to ourselves and to our own sphere of influence. We are like pebbles dropped in a still pond that create ripples that emanate from the splash. We can and do make a difference, whether we are a pebble or a boulder. There is a saying: *no raindrop considers itself to be responsible for the flood.* Yet every drop counts—and so do you.

A note on style: Because of my long career of consulting with dental and orthodontic practices, many of my examples and applications are tailored to those fields. Patient care is often at the forefront. My Messages are equally applicable to the business world, however, and readers who own or manage small companies should be able to easily interpolate to their own businesses and customers. Going a step further, the Messages can even be applied to personal or family life. You will find many quotes throughout my book. This is one of my favorites:

> *One life stamps and influences another, which in turn stamps and influences another, and on and on until the very soul of the human experience breathes on in generations we will never meet.*—**Mary Kay Blakely**

I sincerely hope the messages in this book empower you to be a "raindrop" of love and create a flood of good around you.

Contents

1

Service Talks

Whatever your destiny will be, one thing I know: The only ones among you who will be really happy are those who will have found a way to serve.—**Albert Schweitzer**

The Only Job In Town

Many years ago, when I arrived at a dentist's office for a scheduled consult, I came into the reception area and noticed a sign on the frosty glass window that said, "Ring bell for service." I pushed the button and heard the bell chime. Right behind the window I could make out the form of a woman sitting at the desk but she didn't respond. I rang the bell again—no response. I tapped on the window—still no response.

A few moments later another woman came to the window, reached over the other woman, slid the window aside, and greeted me. I was pleased to be helped finally but vexed when I saw that the woman who had ignored me was *reading a newspaper!* When the consult started, I asked the first woman why she didn't respond to the bell. She answered in a somewhat miffed way, "I'm the hygienist!"

Well, la-de-dah! Besides the obvious fact that she was not a team player, she appeared clueless about what her real job was: to take care of the patients! Not just when they are seated in her operatory chair but in every sense of the word. If the phone is ringing and the front desk staff are busy with other phone calls and patients checking in or out, answer the phone. If the sterilization tech is backed up and the doctor and assistants need more instruments, give a helping hand. Regardless of what your job description specifies, pitch in and do whatever it takes to provide service to the patient.

Another aspect of this "not my job" problem is working alongside someone who thinks her job is so important that everyone else is beneath her. The stress that this attitude alone can cause the rest of the team is staggering. "Team" means *everyone* is aligned on achieving a common goal. In a practice that goal is to take care of the patients, and to do that in such a way that when the patients are walking out the door, they are thinking that the time spent with the practice was the best thing that happened to them that day.

One last note to the story: When I returned to the practice for a follow-up visit, the frosty glass window was gone, as was the "I'm the hygienist!" hygienist. The team was energetic and happy, operating as a unit, and the number of new patients had increased. As John C. Maxwell said, "Teamwork makes the dream work!"

The Power of Empathy

It's been over 55 years since Martin Luther King Jr. awakened countless people with his "I Have A Dream" speech, but racism still persists. Many others, including Mahatma Gandhi, have used the power of empathy to reach into the natural goodness in people and to enroll them in their causes. Daryl Davis, an African-American musician who played with Chuck Berry and Little Richard, has personally converted over 200 Ku Klux Klansmen by befriending them, and in so doing, opened their sense of empathy for African Americans. One Grand Dragon even asked Davis to be his daughter's godfather!

What's this got to do with dentistry? The answer is empathy—your most powerful tool for converting patients into a volunteer sales force! In his book *Customer Empathy*, former TV personality Ross Shafer asserts that customers want more than service—they want a company's employees to view them as more than simply customers. Ross says, "It's thinking about the customers' fears and anxiety, then trying to understand their previous transaction experiences before they met you."

When you put yourself in someone else's shoes, you expand the opportunity for true communication to take place and to serve the person, instead of just "doing your job." If you want patients' cooperation, don't talk *at* them, talk *with* them! In your morning huddle, don't talk patients and procedures—talk about *people*. Use their names and find ways to praise and acknowledge them.

To make this part of the culture of your workplace, start with each other! Treat each other with respect and dignity; speak to people's strengths and talents, especially when under stress or when mistakes are made.

If you want your work environment to be a place where you and others love to be, then make it so! Don't make others wrong—listen from their ears, look from their eyes, and speak from your heart to theirs.

Little Things Mean A Lot

Love is a natural expression of who we are. We feel pleased, even elated, when we experience love in any form, and we feel distressed when it is expected but missing! This is true not only for romantic partners but for patients—they expect "love" in the form of service and appreciation for being a client.

Dr. Steve Hough, a long-time coaching client, and his team exemplify love in action, and his patients greatly appreciate that. Recently, he shared with me feedback from his patients. Here are some samples:

You know, I've been to a lot of doctors over the years and I've become a bit jaded and cynical. But I have to say that you have restored my hope and trust that there are still good doctors that are more focused on taking care of people than just making money.

3

Service Talks

I have been to a lot of doctors and you are the most caring I have ever been to.

You have the most amazing staff!

I asked Steve what he attributes this to, and his answer was "my team." They try to assume the patient's viewpoint and consider what service they would want for themselves or their family. Steve's team brings ideas to him instead of merely waiting for his decisions. Little things matter—like remembering names, making eye-contact, remembering stories or incidents patients shared, and acknowledging any improvement in hygiene or elastics. Make the customer feel like a *person* and not just a customer.

Try viewing your office exactly as your patients might. Are phone calls answered in a pleasant and welcoming way, or must they suffer through a menu of options to find the right person to speak to? As patients enter your office, are they greeted with a smile and welcomed by name? How long do they have to wait before being seen?

Break the Golden Rule!

When I moved back to New York in 2003 to live with my father, I became his primary caretaker. I tried my best to anticipate his needs but often I struck out. The first time he was hospitalized, I brought him framed family photographs and plants from home. "Take those things away!" he commanded. At first, I was shocked and hurt, then I realized my dad didn't want to feel "at home"—he wanted to *go* home. It was a quick lesson in the meaning of real caretaking.

Likewise, in your intent to provide excellent patient care, remember that the patient's view of service is what determines whether you succeed in your goal. The experience of service is so personal. One size does not fit all. Try to listen carefully to patients so they feel welcome and at home!

Monday Morning Messages

Post It!

At least twice a year, my sister Irene comes from Florida to visit me for about two weeks. It is fun for her to stay with me in my home—like revisiting our childhoods in a way. After she's gone, I discover little post-it notes in the most unexpected places: on the pillow, in the bathroom medicine cabinet, in a kitchen drawer, etc. These are little thank-you notes and acknowledgments of my hosting her. On a couple of occasions, I have come across a note a month or more after she's gone! Each one brings a smile to my face and a warm feeling of appreciation for her. And more often than not, they appear at just the right time!

Can you do this with team members or patients? A special little note on a sheet of instructions, an invoice, or staff evaluation might make a real difference—a ray of sunshine to let them know they matter.

Kind words may be short and easy to speak, but their echoes are truly endless.—Mother Teresa

Patient Lessons

Some time ago, I had minor hand surgery but later the wound got infected. After three more surgeries and ten days in the hospital, I learned a lot about being a patient—at the time more than I ever wanted, believe me! But besides leaving with a repaired hand, I left with some valuable lessons about service.

First, most of the hospital workers had really good attitudes. The best example of this was a young employee who cleaned and sterilized my room. Dinesh had a beautiful smile and was proud of her work as a housekeeper. Two things she shared really struck me: If you can't be compassionate with the people in the hospital, you are badly out of place. Second, "hospital" is part of hospitality, something Dinesh lived and breathed in her work. Dinesh stood out to me, but practically every staff person I met had the same attitude.

Service Talks

Health care means working on lives, not just body parts. In dentistry, it is easy to become so focused on the task at hand that service in the larger sense is forgotten. Stay aware of what a patient *experiences*, not just the teeth! Try to personalize the environment. For instance, doctors and assistants wear masks and shields for protection, thus covering half their faces. Help patients feel more comfortable by wearing a photo, like a name tag. Before starting any procedure, explain in detail what is going to happen. If a patient shows poor hygiene, try to engage them with questions rather than admonitions: *What stops you from brushing/flossing/avoiding the wrong foods?* instead of *You need to brush and floss better and avoid junk food.*

The Smile Factor

I really don't like to grocery shop. The stores are nice, clean, and filled with wonderful choices, but I still don't like to shop! I have no choice, though, and trudge off to the store at least twice a week. The last thing I need is grouchy service. Luckily, as I struggle at the self-serve kiosk, a wonderful staff member has come to my rescue. No sooner than the kiosk has chirped "help is on the way," Liz appears and resets the scanner—all the while displaying a beautiful smile! She makes me feel special, even though she treats all her other customers the same way.

Unfortunately, Liz may be more the exception than the rule, not just in this store but in too many retail and professional settings. Smiles don't cost even a penny, yet they reap huge rewards. As a consultant, I very often have had to remind the team and even the doctor that they are in the "smile business." *If you're not wearing a smile, you haven't finished dressing for work!*

Smiles are free face-lifts, free gifts of love!

2

Making a Difference

Never question the power of one! Throughout history it has been the actions of only one person who has inspired the movement of change.—Steve Maraboli

No Problem? No Job!

You are the solution! *To what problem?* you may ask. Well, the only reason you have a job, the only reason *anyone* has a job, is to take care of a problem. Consider all the problems you don't have because someone has come up with the solution to them. For example, when you prepare a meal, you just open the refrigerator, take out some food, and cook it on the stove. You don't have to hunt for your meat, farm the vegetables, or search for wood to build a fire to cook the meal. Others have provided a solution to all of that, giving you lots of time to pursue other things.

Your patients come to you with a problem—they need their teeth fixed. Doctors could do everything by themselves, but then there would be long waiting lists of patients needing treatment. Thus, you are hired to solve the "problems" of answering phones, scheduling appointments, making financial arrangements, sterilizing instruments, ordering supplies, etc., thereby giving the doctor more time to fix teeth and serve more patients. In the end, patients gain confidence, self-esteem, and perhaps a greater likelihood of individual success and happiness.

You may be a cog in a machine, but that machine won't run if that cog isn't working or is missing. Each component is essential to a smoothly running machine.

So it is in life. Don't worry about titles, degrees, or hierarchies. No matter how small a part we may think we play, we can be an important ingredient to the resolution of someone's problem, the answer to someone's prayers and hopes.

Everyone can do simple things to make a difference, and every little bit really does count.— **Stella McCartney**

The Rain Drop

With so much in the news about flooding in towns in the U.S. and across the globe, I was reminded of an old saying: "The rain drop never considers itself responsible for the flood." Yet the flood starts with that single drop!

The same is true in life for both positive and negative changes, and combined with the power of social media, changes can occur like "flash floods."

Like a flood, gossip can sweep away a person's reputation, friends, and even a job. Even before the internet gave rise to cyber-bullying, gossip has always had an energy all its own—as it gains momentum, it can become distorted and multiply the destruction.

On the other hand, floods can have a *positive* effect: One person can influence many others to create a miracle for someone else. Crowd-funding, for example, has saved people from financial ruin; telethons for worthy causes have produced ground swells of support; food drives have stocked soup kitchens and pantries to feed homeless and needy families. Founded in 1982, the Susan B. Komen Breast Cancer Foundation now boasts over 100,000 volunteers in 124 affiliates worldwide and has raised more than $1.5 billion.

One drop—one person—can and does make a difference. In fact, you cannot NOT make a difference. What difference you will make is up to you. Choose wisely!

*Unless someone like you cares a whole awful lot, nothing is going to get better.—***Dr. Seuss**

It's Up To You!

As a coach and consultant, I frequently hear laments from team members about not being appreciated or praised for their work; work not being fun; a general lack of cooperation and too little teamwork. People with these kinds of complaints often feel they have no power to change their situations because they are not the doctor, manager, or supervisor, and thus have no authority to make the changes they want to see. In fact, they are waiting for someone to fix the problem and make them happy.

While I can accept that they lack the authority to make policy changes, that fact does not excuse them from their role in creating a great work environment or a great life!

First of all, you are responsible for your experience of life. You can't control the circumstances, but you have a choice as to how you will respond to them. If you wait for the circumstances to determine your level of peace and happiness, you will be sorely disappointed.

Second, follow the prescription for a happy life: whatever is missing in your life, provide it! If romance is missing in your relationship with your significant other, provide it; if praise and acknowledgement are missing, give it (to yourself and to others); if fun is missing in your work, bring fun with you; if appreciation is missing, show gratitude to and for others.

Finally, follow this rule: Don't let anyone steal your joy! Don't give away your power by letting someone else's mood or behavior negatively impact yours. Positivity is an immunization against an infection of negativity. Make sure that the first thing you do in the morning is to give yourself a healthy dose of self-love, gratitude for all you DO have, and appreciation for all those who DO love you. It's what the happiness doctor orders!

> *It's up to you to be responsible for how you feel if you're not happy. Your happiness lies in your hands.*—**Taraji P. Henson**

9

Making a Difference

You Never Know!

Recently I was speaking with a client who told me that his newest and most enthusiastic team member was a former patient. During the hiring interview he asked her why she wanted to be a clinical assistant. He was surprised by her response. Braces changed her self-image and boosted her self-esteem, but she was also deeply impressed by the way the whole team interacted with her. This planted a seed in her young heart: maybe she too could become someone who could make life better for others while having fun doing it! In fact, she found a career in the dental world that allowed her to make a difference in others' lives.

Often during my seminars I ask participants if any of them chose dentistry or orthodontics as a career because of their experience as a patient. There are *always* many hands raised by both doctors and team members. Always! I know doctors whose former patients not only were inspired to become a dentist or orthodontist, but also specifically wanted to come back to the *same* practice to begin their professional careers. They did, in fact, become an associate or even partner to their original doctor.

It's not necessarily what you do but *how you are being* that really matters. You might never know the impact you will have on those around you! One sure way to keep focused on serving your patients is to start each interaction with a smile. After all, you are in the smile business, and the smile you give may set the tone for that person's day, and maybe even his or her life!

A Different Kind of Labor Day

In late August of 2017, Hurricane Harvey devastated southeast Texas and Louisiana. It was still the major news during the Labor Day weekend, when most people were enjoying a relaxing break from their daily lives. The force of the hurricane, however, assured that an enormous number of people would feel no relief—instead, they were embroiled in a life and death struggle to survive. It would take months before they would return to even a semblance of normalcy, and years before they fully recovered.

Amidst the damage and suffering were countless stories of heroism and unity. Thousands of lives were saved by both the professional first responders and the "neighbor next door." The "Cajun Navy" showed up and started plucking people from their flooded homes. Never once did they ask what ethnicity, religion, gender, sexual preference or political party the victims were. No one asked to be paid—theirs was a labor of love, not of wages or overtime rates. Millions of dollars were raised and organizations around the country sent truckloads of supplies for the recovery effort without specifying who should receive the help. The disaster unified workers, communities were united by the outpouring of humanity.

Still, we don't need a natural disaster to determine our actions or govern our way of relating. We are the creators of our beliefs, and at any moment we can choose peace, charity and kindness. When the waters recede and life begins to return to normal, it is up to us to keep the labels off each other, and to remember our bonds of humanity.

3
Communication

Communication is the real work of leadership.—
Nitin Nohria

Communicate!

I've said it before and I'll say it now: Communication is your most important tool for social control. It determines how you relate to your environment and how others relate to you. Yet too often, when it is most needed is when it is not used, or at least not used effectively. Communication is the answer when there is any kind of a breakdown in any relationship: spouse to spouse; parent to child; sibling to sibling; friend to friend; employer to employee or among employees; and business to its customers.

I will share a personal incident to illustrate the importance of communication and why withholding it only serves to exacerbate the issue. I was in an airport waiting for my flight to Florida when the connecting flight landed and arriving passengers began to deplane. At one point there was a significant pause in the stream of exiting passengers. Several EMTs appeared, navigating a wheelchair holding a woman with an oxygen mask and an IV. They loaded her onto a stretcher and whisked her away.

After the rest of the passengers deplaned, the gate agent finally announced our departing flight would be delayed by four hours! She offered no explanation why, merely adding that we shouldn't go too far from the airport. Puzzled, we passengers were left to speculate as to why. At one point, a passenger came away from the gate desk and informed a few of us that the woman on the stretcher was the flight attendant and she had suffered a heart attack. The flight was delayed because another flight attendant had to be located, and lo and behold, she had to drive all the way from Philadelphia to eastern Long Island! All of this was passed along by word of mouth. Ultimately, the flight was delayed by *six* hours, not four, and never once did the gate agent volunteer any relevant information.

The aggravation and irritation felt by the passengers was due not to the delayed flight, but rather to the fact that the communication was so absent or ineffective. Even the most compassionate and understanding of people lose patience when kept in the dark.

The same is true when dealing with patients. If you are running late, tell them when they arrive, indicate the length of the anticipated delay, and give a reason, if appropriate. This acknowledges that the patient's time is important and allows them the chance to choose how to use it.

Having a problem with a co-worker? Talk to that person! Don't tell others about it and gripe about how good you are and how difficult the other person is. Telling anyone else does not resolve the issue! Afraid to confront the other person? Well don't! Don't confront the person with the issue; confront the issue with the person! Don't know how to do that? Get a neutral third party to mediate the conversation.

Here's the bottom line: No problem can be resolved without communication; with communication, problems disappear.

Learn to Listen and Listen to Learn

There is a famous quote, attributed to both Alan Greenspan and Robert McCloskey, that points out the difficulty and complexity of communication:

> *I know you think you understand what you thought I said but I'm not sure you realize that what you heard is not what I meant.*

The key ingredient in communication breakdowns is that *we don't listen!* We hear, but that doesn't mean we understand.

What we end up responding to is the statement or question that was spoken only in our head, but not out loud.

A communication breakdown can occur on both the speaker's and the listener's sides. Case in point: a woman told her husband that she wanted him to be more romantic. The next day he brought home a bouquet of flowers and a love potion for bedtime. She was not happy. When he complained that he had done what she asked, she said, "I don't want flowers. I want you to offer to give the kids a bath and put them to bed, or take out the trash without being asked." She failed to be specific in her request and he assumed he knew what she meant by "romantic."

This kind of *assumed listening*—that she didn't have to define romantic and he knew what she meant—can be even a bigger problem at work, when people are engaged in routine activities. For instance, the Treatment Coordinator who has "heard it all before" runs the risk of answering questions that are not asked by a new patient, thus appearing insincere as she goes through her routine. The same is true for any team member who doesn't *stop!* and make real contact with the patient. For example, when giving instructions for hygiene and follow-up, it is critical that you "listen" before you speak by paying attention to the "person" instead of a "patient."

Learn to listen and listen to learn. This never fails, every time it's tried!

> *There is a difference between listening and waiting for your turn to speak.*—**Simon Sinek**

Labels and Limits

It is a natural and normal characteristic that we label almost everything in life. It allows us to create a semblance of order for ourselves and an understanding among people. For instance, I can say "doctor" or "patient" or "team" and immediately these labels elicit mental pictures and emotional responses in the listener, creating a common ground of understanding.

The pitfall of labeling occurs when we assume the label "says it all" and we don't delve further to see the impact the label has on our actions and interactions. Some labels are not as obviously negative or damaging, and do serve as a basis for clarity in communication. For instance, there is nothing "bad" about calling someone a "patient" in speaking with each other in a team meeting, as in "we need to take care of our patients." However, in the morning huddle, it's important to reference patients by name rather than by diagnosis, for example: "We have a new patient exam at 1:00" versus "Tommy Jones is 13 years old and is looking forward to his exam at 1:00. The label tends to *depersonalize* whereas individualizing the person enhances the relationship before he even walks in the door.

While I am not suggesting that you totally abandon the use of labels, I am urging you to go beyond the label and see the person as an individual. Do whatever you can to enhance the sense of connection you have with each other and with those you want to serve.

> *Labels are for filing. Labels are for clothing. Labels are not for people.*—**Martina Navratilova**

Stress Less

At one time or another, every practice encounters problems that can be stressful—emergency walk-ins, team members out sick, patients coming in late, and equipment breakdowns. These glitches can throw people off their game and create stress.

We know how stress feels: general tension in the body, an increased heart rate, a widening of the eyes. Mostly we assign the source of stress to circumstances, and once the circumstances change, we assume the stress will go away.

It is natural to feel stress when you are behind schedule and patients are becoming impatient! Worrying about it, though, can cause more tension, which leads to mistakes that can put you further behind. You can break this vicious cycle through communication. Make sure the receptionist lets patients know how long a delay they can expect and give them the option of rescheduling. If you are stuck in traffic and will be late, call ahead

The most important communication is the one you are having with yourself that is forecasting failure. Decide that failure is neither a given nor an option. If there is something you can do to change the situation, then do that. If not, then admit that fretting and fuming only change your sense of well-being.

Keep your focus on the goal, switch gears, and go to Plan B when necessary.

Word Power

Have you ever noticed how some words have such power as to make your stomach turn or your body to tense up? Hear the word *no* and your body changes slightly, just as is does when you hear the word *yes.* The words we toss out without thinking *do* matter and can either support your intention to communicate or undermine it.

For instance, telling someone you're *very angry* has a stronger effect on the listener than saying *I'm annoyed.* Words carry an intensity with them—try to dial down. It is easier for someone to hear *I'm concerned* than *I'm really worried.* Likewise, someone is less likely to get defensive if you say *I'm bothered* rather than *I'm angry.*

The point of communication is to "come together" and when you use high intensity words, you hamper real communication and create distance between you and the other person. Start to notice the words you use, and as you raise your awareness, start choosing words that express the meaning you want to convey without creating defensive listening.

Communication

On a personal note, I have made a commitment to stop using the word *hate*—the word's intensity is so high that it increases stress levels in both the speaker and the listener. In addition, it is rarely true. I hear people say they hate to go to work, then wonder why their moods are so sour for the day. Changing that statement to "I'd prefer to be at the beach/home/golfing" is more relaxing and positive.

Angry versus annoyed, worried versus concerned, hate versus dislike. If one sounds easier on your ears than the other, then remember to make it easy for you to be heard! Words have power. Choose yours wisely!

It Takes Two to Argue!

A client recently asked me to mediate a problem between two of his team members. As is always the case, both people had their version of what had happened and insisted that what they did and said was justifiable. In a way, both were right, considering their own viewpoints, yet neither was happy about the situation.

The difficulty in resolving disputes is letting go of your point of view long enough to allow yourself to see the other person's perspective. Stubbornness may set in when both parties insist they are right. Let go of your need to be right! Put things in perspective: Is the issue really worth having to avoid contact with that person when you're working side by side for eight hours, or worth disrupting harmony in the practice?

The words *I apologize* open the door to healing and restoration. Usually when one party steps up and takes responsibility for his or her own behavior, the other person does the same. Regardless of the other person's response to the apology, be the hero in the matter. Be the person you want others to admire and the person who at the end of the day looks at him or herself in the mirror and says, "I'm proud of you!"

Doing the Do

My parents always admonished us kids that "actions speak louder than words" as a reminder that we were judged by what we do and not so much by what we say. This universal truth is particularly true in establishing loyalty and trust in relationships.

Whenever I work with a doctor and team, I always ask to see their mission statement. More often than not, no one can say what it is, and just as likely, they have a hard time *finding* it. The mission statement needs to be readily accessible, because it sets up expectations for the patients and states the standards by which the doctor's and the team's performance will be judged. If your actions don't match up with your words, you risk losing trust with the patient.

Find your mission statement and if you don't have one, create it! What are the key words in it that reflect your core values? Choose one each week to focus on, and in the morning huddles, decide ways your behaviors can and will reflect that value. This applies not only to your interactions with the patients and families, but also among the team. It's critical that your relationships with each other demonstrate the core values in order for your patients to view you as being authentic.

> *A mission statement is not something you write overnight. But fundamentally, your mission statement becomes your constitution, the solid expression of your vision and values.*—**Stephen Covey**

The Art of Listening

You've heard the phrase: *"God gave us two ears and one mouth for a reason!* This means more than just not talking when someone else is speaking; and listening is not simply hearing and understanding the spoken word. It means to stop formulating in your head what your response will be when the other person stops speaking. It means to be willing to be in the other person's shoes—to see what he sees, to feel what she feels, to allow the other person to speak without judgment.

Unfortunately, this does not come naturally for most people. If it did, there would be fewer arguments and more collaboration. To listen openly does not mean you have to agree with what is being said, but rather that you respect another's right to disagree. It also allows for your responses to maintain dignity for both you and the other person. Without listening there can be no communication; there can only be speaking and hearing.

The art of listening reaps rewards beyond simply avoiding arguments. It is the essence of great leadership and the heart of effective marketing. Imagine yourself as a customer who is dissatisfied with a product and service, and when you register your complaint with the company, that company's representative listens to you instead of explaining why you had that problem, or worse yet, treats you as if *you* are the problem!

The same is true if you are an employee on the receiving side of a corrective conversation or the person giving the correction. All feelings of guilt, blame or embarrassment will disappear, and what is left is a positive step toward change and a feeling of satisfaction.

Keep your focus on the end result you want: peace and satisfaction!

We have but two ears and one mouth so that we may listen twice as much as we speak.—**Thomas Edison**

Words Can Change Your Life

I recently read a story of Jennifer Bricker, a young woman who was born without legs, and whose mother abandoned her at birth. Her adoptive parents raised her as if she were a normal child who could do anything she wanted. She wanted to be just like her idol, Olympic gymnast Dominique Moceanu. "Can't" was never part of Jennifer's vocabulary.

She started at age seven on a trampoline. Soon she was competing and then dominating. By high school, Jennifer Bricker was tumbling champion of the state of Illinois!

"There isn't a disabled tumbling division," revealed Jen, who competed against able-bodied athletes. "At that time and probably still today, I was the only handicapped person to ever compete in power tumbling." An amazing postscript to this story is that Jennifer did meet Dominique and they discovered they are biological sisters!

There are hundreds of stories about people who have severe disabilities yet achieve success beyond anyone's expectations or beliefs about what was possible for them. The common denominator in these stories is that these people refuse to believe *I can't* and instead focus on what they *can* do.

It would be wonderful if we all had parents and teachers and mentors in our childhoods who supported us with positive messages and reinforced our capabilities rather than pointed out our mistakes or lack of ability. But as adults, we must take responsibility for managing our self-talk and training ourselves to believe in ourselves and be our own best mentors. To paraphrase what Henry Ford said, if you believe you can, you will, and if you believe you can't, you won't. From here on, be the coach you always wanted, and cheer yourself on to victory!

Right/Wrong—Win/Lose

Life is both complex and simple. The simplicity of it is in the circumstances of life that are constant—weather and climate, war, poverty, and crime. The complexity comes from the fact that we humans have a number of possible responses to the circumstances. The key word is *responses*. If we simply react to a situation, then we are subject to the "fight or flight" mechanism, and very little, if any, thinking is involved. On the other hand, a response involves a conscious choice—thinking about and evaluating possible outcomes.

The best opportunity to *choose* your response is when speaking with someone who disagrees with your point of view, especially when you are feeling verbally attacked. What we "hear" when someone disagrees with us is *One of us is wrong, and it's not me!* The person may never actually say the words *you're wrong!* but instead it is the person's tone of voice or facial expression or body language that says it. If you immediately react *I am not!* you will become deadlocked. The more you push, the harder the pushback.

Win-lose is acceptable in sports, but in human relationships, it's win-win or else lose-lose. The way to create win-win is first to change how you listen to "different." Different isn't wrong, it is simply different! In fact, different is what creates progress and growth. When you embrace "different" as non-threatening, you create a space of possibility for conflict resolution, for strengthening bonds of friendship and teamwork, and for growth and new ideas.

Understanding that everyone has their own experience of life—their own circumstances and viewpoints—and accepting that these are just as valid as yours, creates a sense of respect and dignity for them. This lays the foundation for communication!

> *Adopt a new philosophy of cooperation (win-win) in which everybody wins.*—W. Edwards Deming

Impact of Words

My mother had a subscription to Reader's Digest for as long as I can remember, and the most recent issue was always in plain view. In addition to the stories and essays, the magazine had regular features in every issue, such as "Military Humor." (*The new army rifle weighs 7.6 lbs, but after carrying it for a couple of miles, the decimal point drops out!*) My mother's favorite, "Word Power," helped you add to your vocabulary to impress others. The magazine's influence was always apparent when my mother came up with phrases such as: *You have the unmitigated gall to tell me . . . .*

Albert Mehrabian's research in interpersonal communication in 1967 included rule 7-38-55: Our interpretation of the meaning of a spoken message is 7% on the actual word, 38% on the sound and intonation of the word, and 55% on the visual aspects, such as body language, gestures and facial expressions. Though this is likely true, it's not the entire picture.

Words do have power! We like the word *yes* and dislike *no*—a word no one likes to hear and many people even have trouble saying. It's important to be aware that many words elicit strong emotional reactions. Be especially aware of this when you need to communicate being upset to someone. If you want resolution, collaboration, and cooperation, choose your words wisely. For instance, instead of saying *angry,* use the word *"annoyed"* to lessen the intensity of what you are saying and create less defensiveness for the listener.

Using the less dramatic word also eases your own body language and facial expressions and again, opens up the space for listening. Some other examples of word substitutions are: *sometimes* instead of *always* or *never; uncomfortable* instead of *painful; sad* instead of *devastated.*

The suggestions above won't guarantee smooth sailing in your communications, but they will definitely calm the waters!

> *Whatever words we utter should be chosen with care, for people will hear them and be influenced by them for good or ill.*—Buddha

Dead Plants and Other Give-Aways

Erma Bombeck was a humorist, author and columnist who was famous for her witty outlook on suburban home life during the 1960s-90s. One of my favorite quips by her is:

Communication

"Never go to a doctor whose office plants have died." A short sentence with volumes of wisdom packed into it.

Years ago, I was consulting with a dentist and had been to his office to observe for a couple of hours. When we met that evening to review my findings, I acknowledged him for the lovely appearance of his newly remodeled office. I also mentioned that he should remove the dead plant in a corner of the reception area as it sent the wrong message: We don't take care of living things! I suggested he remove it and give it to someone who has a green thumb, then hire a rent-a-plant company to "seed" his office.

Keep in mind, EVERY thing communicates! One of the basic tenets of effective communication is making sure that what you say matches the tone of your voice, your facial expressions, and your body language. In fact, the visual aspect of communication carries the majority of meaning in a communication, to the point that it's possible to convey a strong message without saying a word.

When words don't match tone of voice or the visual aspects of a communication, the speaker is considered to be inauthentic. If you are promoting your practice or business to be committed to excellence, make sure everything reflects that. Here are some real-life examples of practices that missed the mark: a treatment coordinator who needs braces; team members who show up looking like they just rolled out of bed; uniforms that fit poorly or need ironing; reception room magazines that are torn from use and are outdated; chairs in the operatory or reception area that have tears or stains on them; trash cans that need to be emptied; burnt-out light bulbs; messy labs; and the proverbial dead plant!

Here's a simple exercise: Have everyone take a pad and pen and start outside in the parking lot. Each person should write down anything and everything they see that is "off" or in need of repair or attention. In effect, do a walk-through of the office as if you are making up a punch list with a contractor before you take ownership. Create a master list from everyone's observations, then a To Do list with a timeline and the person responsible for each task. Make this part of your annual review.

> **Excellence is doing ordinary things extraordinarily well.**—John William Gardner

Just the Facts

In the late 1960s there was a popular TV crime series called Dragnet, and the main character, Sgt. Joe Friday, would always instruct witnesses: "Just the facts, ma'am (sir), just the facts." Friday needed to separate people's emotional interpretations of events from the actual occurrences in order to solve the crimes. There is what actually happened, and then there a person's *interpretation* of what happened.

Unlike real life crime drama, with witness testimonies being scrutinized the way Sgt. Friday did, our normal, everyday conversations are often rife with our own interpretation of events and people but are spoken as if they are facts.

An assessment is how one feels or interprets something, whereas an assertion is the fact of the matter. For instance, if you say, *It's a beautiful day,* that is an assessment, but *It's daytime and the temperature is 80 degrees with mostly sunshine and a few clouds* is an assertion.

Assessments are neither good nor bad, they just *are.* They are not facts but instead are personal interpretations. If you make an assessment and then back it up with facts, that is an assertion. Be mindful of how much of our own interpretation or "spin" we place on the subjects we are discussing. This is especially true when we speak about situations when we are coaching, correcting, or passing information on to others. For example, we can say: *Johnny is a difficult patient. He doesn't floss and he breaks brackets.* In fact, we don't *know* if Johnny is a "difficult patient"—that is an assessment. That he doesn't floss is an assertion. The team member might have had difficulty convincing Johnny to floss and take care of his brackets, but charting *Johnny is difficult* might presuppose a subsequent team member to the same assessment. By the same token, *Johnny is a great patient* also is an assessment that needs to be backed up by facts. In either case, the first team assessment colors the second one.

"Just the facts, ma'am," clears up mysteries and supports healthy relationships.

4
Attitude of Gratitude

Gratitude can transform common days into thanksgivings, turn routine jobs into joy, and change ordinary opportunities into blessings.—**William Arthur Ward**

Seeing With the Eyes of Innocence

There is an old story about a rich man who wanted to teach his son the difference between how rich and poor people live, intending to teach the son how fortunate he was. He takes his son on a trip to a rural area that is considered to be poor. After the visit, the father asks his son what he learned. His son's responses were not at all what the father expected:

> *I saw that we have one dog and they had four. We have a pool that reaches to the middle of our garden and they have a creek that has no end. We have imported lanterns in our garden and they have the stars at night. Our patio reaches to the front yard and they have the whole horizon. We have a small piece of land to live on and they have fields that go beyond our sight. We have servants who serve us, but they serve others. We buy our food, but they grow theirs. We have walls around our property to protect us, and they have friends to protect them.*

The boy's father was speechless.

Then his son added, *Thanks Dad, for showing me how poor we are.*

We can glean several points from this story:

Attitude of Gratitude

Circumstances just "are," and it is our interpretation of those circumstances that determine how they are to us!

"Rich" and "poor" are labels we've made up and are only an interpretation.

Appreciation and gratitude are a function of our interpretation as well.

At any given moment, regardless of the circumstances, we can find something for which we are grateful. Modify your interpretation and experience true appreciation.

Feeling stressed because you are busy at work? Thank goodness you are busy or you wouldn't be in business, or wouldn't have a job.

Stuck in traffic? At least you have a car.

Tired of housework? What a blessing to have a home to keep up.

Two men looked out from prison bars. One saw the mud, the other saw the stars.—Dale Carnegie

Contrasts

Noted web designer John O'Nolan defines *contrast* as "things which look different from one another." Contrast is a fundamental tool for design, as it allows things to be distinguished from each other, providing impact as well as visual interest and emphasis.

In other words, contrast is a good thing in life, too! Unfortunately, we don't value contrast as much when it comes to the ups and downs of life. In fact, we label the ups and downs as good and bad, or right and wrong, and our happiness and attitudes seesaw along with the changes.

While this is the "normal" pattern of life, our assessments of right/wrong and good/bad end up determining our attitudes and our behaviors. What we overlook is that the ups and downs provide us contrast and the possibility of deepening appreciation, gratitude, and learning. We strive to make sure we are always "happy" by eliminating all problems.

Don't get me wrong. I'm not suggesting we should not strive to eliminate problems. In fact, I believe the purpose of all work is eliminating some existing problem. What I am asserting is that our attitude and moods need to be independent of the ups and downs of life, and that we should be using the contrast of ups and downs to deepen our gratitude and appreciation for life in general. Being happy is a state of mind—a choice we make regardless of the circumstances. Those who embrace this axiom of life are the ones who become most successful in whatever they do.

My friend Linda Miles is one of the most successful consultants and speakers in the dental community. Her career has spanned decades and has changed the lives of many doctors and their team members and patients. Linda didn't start off that way. She grew up in a small West Virginia town, married Don, her high school sweetheart, when she was eighteen and struggled to make ends meet and raise their two children. Yet through all the lean years, she and Don were happy! Their appreciation for life kept deepening through every obstacle and problem they encountered. In fact, she used the struggles to keep broadening her commitment to others and to making a contribution to life in general.

Right now you may be in one of the valleys of life—*be happy anyway!* You may be at the top of the hill—*be happy!* You may be on the downslope heading south—*be happy!* Whatever your current struggle, convince yourself to experience happiness. Look around you. You're on the right side of the grass and it's green!

Attitude of Gratitude

The Garden of Your Mind

When spring arrives in the northeast, I delight in the daffodils and tulips and all the blooms that are beginning to show their full beauty.

But just as the flowers are coming into their own, so are the weeds! In fact, they seem to thrive even more than the flowers and threaten to take over the garden beds. Every planting season, the job of gardening seems to be increasingly defined by weeding. I pull the weeds to the roots, then scatter a pre-emergent weed killer and cover the beds in mulch to further suppress the weeds, all with the goal of providing a bed that nurtures my flowers.

To me, gardening is a great metaphor for maintaining a positive attitude and perspective on life. Negative thoughts, poor attitudes, and low self-esteem are weeds that can overtake the beauty inherent in all of us. They need to be uprooted and discarded, then replaced with the "proper fertilizer" to grow a healthy attitude.

When you start thinking, "I'm not good enough, smart enough, pretty enough, or young enough," that's the moment you have to stop, pull the thought out by the roots, and replace it with beautiful thoughts about yourself. Notice who loves you, who is proud of you, who believes in you, and bring those thoughts to the forefront of your mind. An attitude of gratitude will be the fertilizer that will also prevent the "weeds" from returning. Be grateful for both the sun and the rain; for a job that provides meaningful work; and for all you *can* do.

All summer long, I keep checking the garden beds to see if any weeds have popped up through the mulch, then I pull them out. The mulch doesn't stop the weeds altogether but it does slow down their emergence—the job gets easier in time. In like manner, tending the garden of your mind requires vigilance and on-going work, but in time the job gets easier. Ultimately, the garden blooms with beauty!

Get Even!

"What?!" No, I'm not promoting revenge as an interpersonal strategy. Instead, I am suggesting that you "get even" with those who love you.

If you take notice, every day you are surrounded by people who let you know you are important, appreciated and loved. There may not be dramatic expressions of support each day, but it's really up to you to recognize even the smallest and quietest statements that come your way. Did someone take out the trash for you, give you a hug, ask you *How are you doing?* Do not mistake these as being mundane and unimportant. Too often we take these acts for granted instead of enjoying the "wow" moments.

The best thing to do is to take it a step further and "get even" with the people who love you. Don't wait for the special occasion or holiday to let the people in your life know you love and appreciate them. Leave a small note in your children's lunch box or backpack that simply says, "I'm proud of you!" Surprise your spouse with a special night off—let them know that everything is handled and they can do whatever they want without worrying about chores or duties. Have each of your family members let you know what their favorite meal is and plan the night to have it, complete with a special badge that says "King" or "Queen" for the day. Send a thank-you note to a team member for "going the extra mile" for you or the patients.

The more you "get even," the more you will be wowed in your life.

Gratitude is not only the greatest of virtues, but the parent of all others.—Cicero

Meaningful Mistakes

Mistakes happen. It is the meaning we give to our mistakes that really matters. A common immediate reaction to an error is to cover up the mistake and hope no one notices.

Attitude of Gratitude

But if someone does observe our mistake and calls us out, the second response is to explain and justify the mistake, and blame others for it. Neither of these responses produces a desirable result; in fact, both almost guarantee that the mistake will be repeated.

On the positive side, mistakes are part of the learning process. A child learns balance and how to walk by falling down. Of course, history is filled with examples of how people failed before achieving success. Henry Ford failed and went broke five times before he succeeded. R.H. Macy failed seven times before his store in New York caught on. Thomas Edison tried a *thousand* different materials and combinations until he found the right filament that created the light bulb. When Edison was asked by a reporter how it felt to fail 1000 times, he replied, "I didn't *fail* 1000 times, the light bulb was an invention with 1000 steps." In every case, these successes came from a powerful interpretation: There is always something to learn that can and will further the person's growth and achievements.

Instead of trying to hide your mistakes, look for what you can learn from the mistake and then share it with your teammates. When someone corrects you for a mistake, don't make excuses or justify yourself. Thank the person and collaborate with them in the future.

Labor and Love

There is an old saying, *Do what you love and you'll never work a day in your life.* It is a great sentiment and surely has at least *some* truth to it. If you love what you do, it will never seem like labor or drudgery we often associate with the concept of work.

One of my favorite TV reality shows was *Undercover Boss.* What I valued about it was the number of employees in various companies, in various jobs, who loved what they did despite low pay, long hours, poor working conditions, or demanding customers and bosses. They truly had an "attitude of gratitude" and focused on serving customers instead of complaining about their jobs. One female electrician was asked by the undercover boss how she managed such a great attitude despite her poor working conditions, low pay, and no praise. She responded that none of those issues had anything to do with the customers, so why would she make them pay for her problems with the company? (Eventually, during the program's "reveal," she got a significant raise and a promotion, plus working conditions for all employees were improved significantly!)

Employees on *Undercover Boss* all reported, in one way or the other, loving their jobs, even though there were lots of things they didn't even like about their work. Conversely, of course, many people with high-paying jobs in lovely surroundings, great benefits, and lots of prestige seem endlessly disgruntled at work.

When you contrast these opposite scenarios, it becomes obvious that we always have a choice about how we are going to BE at work—or anywhere in life for that matter! If we allow circumstances to dictate our mood, we actually give up our own power and risk feeling victimized by the whims of the day. Work becomes drudgery, something to escape from, and people end up passing their misery on to others.

Choose to love what you do. There will always be things about work and your job that you don't like, just as there are things that you love. Focus on the end result rather than the immediate problem. Satisfaction and happiness are choices. Choose well!

What do we live for if not to make life less difficult for each other?—George Eliot

Attitude of Gratitude

In Joy

When asked what they want in their lives, most people put "to be happy" at the top of their list. Of course, what makes people happy varies from person to person. But the source of happiness is the same for all of us: JOY! It is such a natural state for human beings that you can even see it in infants and small children as they begin to discover the world around them: rolling over or pulling themselves up for the first time; taking their first steps; recognizing their mommy and daddy when they come into the room, and countless other milestones achieved in the process of growing up.

Somewhere along the way, this "joy for just being alive" starts to fade and human *beings* turn into human *doings*. Instead of simply experiencing joy and love around us, we end up doing things to try to get them. It's like looking for your glasses when you're wearing them!

What has this got to do with an orthodontic practice, or with *any* business for that matter? Ask yourself: If you had to go to a doctor or a dentist, or go shopping for something, would you rather go where the people were glad to be there and appreciated their job and coworkers, or where people simply "punched in and punched out," waiting for the work week to go away and the paycheck to arrive?

To quote noted international speaker and author Amanda Gore, "Joy is an inside job!" Bring your joy with you to work and even burdensome chores become lighter. Tap into your own pool of joy and it will nurture joy in others. Your spark might light up their day.

Joy is free advertising, speaking louder than any paid ad, coupon, or gimmick used to lure people to a business. It is the language of the heart: Once expressed, it cannot be muted, and its sound will echo in the chambers of the hearts of all who hear it.

Life is like a mirror—it reflects back to you what you bring to it. You get joy and satisfaction from your work and life because you bring it with you to start! When you keep looking for the good in life, when you seek to spread your joy, you will reap the rewards of happiness and love. Always, be *In Joy!*

Love What You Do—Do What You Love

In 1970, Stephen Stills penned a hit song, "Love The One You're With." The catch phrase in the chorus was, *And if you can't be with the one you love, love the one you're with.* Not exactly great advice for someone in a monogamous relationship, but the essence of the message has value. Consider: Almost two decades later, Marsha Sinetar wrote a book called *Do What You Love and the Money Will Follow.* What a gem of advice! Combine it with Stills' urging and you might find the blueprint for success in your own life.

Most of the people I work with are in the orthodontic/dental community and can joyfully assert they have their dream job. They do work that makes a difference in a pleasant workspace with other caring individuals. They earn healthy salaries and enjoy good benefits and work hours that allow ample time to spend with family and friends. Despite all of this, not everyone is happy at work, and that's not really surprising. We have a human tendency to always be looking at what we don't have rather than appreciating what we do have.

In every walk of life, the people who rise above the rest are those who look at life as an opportunity and an adventure in learning. Even obstacles and "failures" are used as stepping stones towards their goals. They stay focused on what is working and build on that.

Focus is the key. Life doesn't go as planned. Unexpected problems arise. Make the most of what is in front of you. Do you have a problem patient or a problem with a co-worker? How can you use the situation to develop patience, improve your negotiating skills, or deepen your understanding of others? When you meet with difficulties, try to find "the silver lining" and to be grateful for all that you do have.

If you love what you do, it isn't your job, it is your love affair.—**Debasish Mridha**

Time Flies

The annual meeting of the American Association of Orthodontists that I attended in San Diego in 2017 marked the thirty-first year I've been involved with orthodontics, and the twenty-fifth time I've spoken at the convention. I am forever thankful for my winding career path that brought me to the world of orthodontics and dentistry in general.

On the flight home I had time to reflect on my decades-long involvement with this incredibly rewarding profession. It sure doesn't feel like thirty-plus years have passed, and it reminds me of the adage, *Time flies when you are having a good time.* But it goes way beyond enjoyment for me when I add up the number of states I've traveled to (47), the countries I've visited (4), the continents I've been to (3), and more importantly, the countless number of friends I've made along the way!

In fact, I am profoundly moved by the difference that being a part of the "smile industry" has made in my life, as it has deepened my sense of compassion and empathy for people. I so enjoy seeing patients' lives transformed when their smiles are restored and their confidence soars. And I feel grateful knowing I have played a small part in transforming the outlook of many in orthodontics and dentistry from "I've *gotta* go to work," to "I *get* to go to work!"

Whatever your work experience is, whether you are a "newbie" or a seasoned pro, whether you are the doctor or a team member, the benefits your profession has afforded you go way beyond the amount of your paycheck, and in many ways, mirror the experiences I have shared here. It's an important and valuable exercise to lift our heads out of the immediate moment and reflect on the journey that brought us to this "now." I suggest you create a list at your morning huddle by having each person write down on a flip chart what benefits this marvelous profession has afforded them. Keep adding to the list and discover for yourselves how orthodontics and dentistry have impacted your life.

To find joy in work is to discover the fountain of youth.—Pearl S. Buck

Think Thanks Every Day

In 1863, Abe Lincoln proclaimed the last Thursday in November to be a day to give thanks after a relentless campaign by Sarah Josepha Hale, editor of *Godey's Lady's Book*, who had been petitioning politicians for thirty-six years! However, it wasn't until 1941 that Congress created the fourth Thursday in November to be a national holiday.

It's always a good idea to take time to acknowledge all the good in your life, not just on holidays and special occasions, but every day and even often during the day. In the busy and hectic pace of life, it's easy to get caught up in the swirl of negativity that surrounds us. Life is filled with problems, and despite our wishing that problems would just go away, they also give meaning to our lives. Businesses are actually based on creating solutions to problems. If there is no problem, there is no reason for a business to exist! (And if everyone had perfectly aligned teeth, there would be no need for orthodontists!)

Very smart entrepreneurs, like Steve Jobs, created solutions to problems customers didn't know they had until they saw an iPod or an iPhone and realized that they had been "making do" with CD players and flip phones, now outdated. But in their time, CD players and flip phones were also solutions to problems invented by the patent holders!

Being thankful is actually an attitude, an interpretation of circumstances, a point of view of life that transforms life

Attitude of Gratitude

itself! Thus, a person who has amassed great wealth and "has everything" can be miserable and depressed, while a person struggling to make ends meet is happy and approaches each day as an opportunity to love and to experience joy. Focusing on gratitude is not a guarantee that your problems will go away, but an *attitude of gratitude* will empower you to deal with your problems in a more productive way.

5
Teamwork

I can do things you cannot. You can do things I cannot. Together we can do great things.— **Mother Teresa**

It Takes Confidence to be Humble

On my safari in the Mala Mala Game Reserve in South Africa, I was struck by the elegant service everyone at the reserve provided us. At some point, it occurred to me that there was an element of humility among the staff. I was curious why humility should be the trait to stand out for me when associated with service.

Humility is commonly defined as "the quality or state of not thinking you are better than other people," or "a modest or low view of one's own importance." Antonyms of the word include arrogance, egotism, and haughtiness. What was not addressed in the definitions was that it takes a great sense of self-confidence to be humble, to be so clear about your talents that using these for serving others is joyous. In fact, the phrase *it's a pleasure to serve you* is resoundingly authentic.

I noticed the staff at Mala Mala afforded the same sense of service to one another as well. They always addressed each other by name, said "please" and "thank you" consistently, offered help to each other, and did whatever was necessary to ensure that they, as well as the guests, had a stress-free and enjoyable day. Interestingly, every employee actually lives at the camp for 4–6 weeks at a time before having two weeks off. Wouldn't living together while working together bring on *more* "personality conflicts" and opportunities for breakdowns in teamwork? Apparently not!

Teamwork

When my travel companion and I asked about how workers manage conflict and maintain such great relationships, our ranger told us that difficulties are handled *immediately,* and everyone tries to stay focused on their true purpose. They don't compete with each other, they collaborate. No one is more important than anyone else, regardless of job title or responsibilities. They know and understand that each person is vital to creating an exceptional experience for their guests, whether they are the rangers who take the guests on the rides into the bush or the people who prepare meals and clean rooms. There is no hierarchy of importance among the team but rather a commitment to creating an unforgettable experience of the joy of service. Everyone counts equally.

Is there competition among *your* team? A lack of regard for others' jobs? Have you lost focus on why you have a job? If so, then let go of egotism and arrogance, communicate respectfully to clear problems up before they fester, and stay focused on making your patients feel special and appreciated. At the end of the day, you will feel better about a task well performed, and your patients will be grateful, even if they don't express it!

The Stress Factor

When you read the word "stress" you probably think of pressure, lack of time, or anxiety about some situation. There is, however, another meaning that has a lot of power in assisting you in achieving your goals and just being happier in life. This other meaning is "emphasis" or "focus." What do you attend to most, not only consciously but unconsciously? It's interesting to note that what you *stress* can actually stress you!

Case in point: I was working with an orthodontic team and one of their main concerns was how to deal with late or no-show patients. At some point in the discussion, I asked them for the average number of their patients who are either late or no-shows on a given day. They said three or four. So, in the course of a four-day week (the fifth day being a non-patient day for them) that would make sixteen, seemingly a significant number. However, they see an average of eighty patients a day, so the number of late or no-show patients is only 5%, with 95% of the patients coming on time! Yet, the team seemed to place 80–90% of their focus on the 5% who were late.

By no means do I think they should just brush off the problem as trivial. But do I think they were making it a bigger deal than necessary? Yes. The real problem in this scenario is that while they focused on the late arrivals, they were taking their focus off patients who *were* on time. As they stressed the problem of tardiness of patients, they stressed themselves out!

In many languages, a stress mark indicates what syllable to emphasize. Consider where your practice or business is placing its accent marks. And to quote my mother, "Put the acCENT on the right syl-LAB'le!"

What you stay focused on will grow.—Roy T. Bennett

E Pluribus Unum

E pluribus unum—translated from Latin, it means "out of many, one." The United States has claimed this tenet as perhaps its most sacred founding principle, because it represents the melding of many different peoples and cultures into a single great country. The whole is far greater than its parts.

On a different level, *e pluribus unum* applies to teams of all kinds, including your work team. The source of success is a disparate group of people, with various talents, backgrounds, viewpoints, and experiences, aligning in purpose and mission. These differences become assets, not problems or points of irritation. When a group is unified on a mission, they produce results that exceed what any one person or one type of person could produce. On the other hand, teams fall apart when individual differences are denigrated rather than respected, or when personality styles, traits and aptitudes are treated as *wrong* rather than *different*, or when they stop honoring the contribution these differences make to the success of the whole. "From many, one" is a statement of inclusion that also implies respect and appreciation for the differences.

Communication promotes teamwork and respect

As the French saying goes, *Vive la différence!*

Marching to the Beat

Everyone has heard the phrase that someone *marched to the beat of a different drummer.* We often admire such "drummers," especially those inventors, pioneers, and creators of new horizons—explorers who defy norms to discover better pathways for themselves and society.

The United States is replete with such "renegades"— Abraham Lincoln, Thomas Edison, Marie Curie, Martin Luther King Jr, George Washington Carver, Susan B. Anthony, Rosa Parks, and Henry Ford, for example. They represent different fields and eras, but each of them "interrupted" the way things were and blazed a new trail for the future.

Orthodontics, too, has had its fair share of innovators. One of the first was Edward Angle, who founded the American Association of Orthodontists in 1901. From there, treatment techniques took quantum leaps during the 20th century when banding every tooth went to bonding brackets on teeth to the current innovations of aligners and a vast array of brackets and wires, all unheard of seventy years ago.

On the "soft side" of orthodontics, a major shift occurred in the early 1980s when the idea of a Treatment Coordinator was introduced. There was initial resistance: Many believed that only doctors could adequately present the case findings to their patients. Now, thirty years later, most doctors realize that Treatment Coordinators can establish relationships and communicate with patients much better than the doctor can or has time for. This change in the structure of the consult has produced breakthroughs in the doctor's ability to serve patients and grow the practice simultaneously.

The truth is we all have a drum to beat. When you hire on to a practice, you agree to beat your drum in unison with the band so that you create great music together. If you are the doctor and own a practice, hire people who can march in step and enhance the power and reach of your "music"!

> *There is immense power when a group of people with similar interests work toward the same goals.*—Idowu Koyenikan

Suckatude

On a recent flight, I sat next to another speaker on his way to a meeting and in our conversation, I learned a new word: *suckatude*! I laughed and immediately got what he was talking about. As my seatmate pointed out, suckatude is the mood someone has that will suck the energy and positivity out of a room full of people.

When I got to my hotel room, I Googled the word and found its definition in the Urban Dictionary: *a poor attitude in life. "His suckatude was ruining everyone's good time."* The word was new to me, but it's apparently been around for a while. Even more interesting was the second definition: *An unhealthy situation. "The delinquents often hurt themselves instead of pulling themselves out of their suckatude."*

Teamwork

It was this latter definition that gave me pause. We all know that someone with a bad attitude can bring down others, but we don't normally look at that person and conclude that they are unhealthy. Instead, the tendency is to flee—create distance from them. But if we know someone is physically sick, we encourage them to get medical treatment or at least take better care of themselves. We also protect ourselves from catching a contagious disease. What we don't do is allow the person to infect others. So why do we allow negativity to infect ourselves and others? Why not treat it with the same compassion and intent as we do with physical ailments?

There is a big difference between physical sickness and emotional attitudes, of course, especially in social acceptability. For instance, if someone is physically ill, it's okay to offer assistance and make suggestions for improving one's health. But if it's an emotional issue, it becomes "none of your business." Except it *is* others' business if a co-worker's attitude is damaging team spirit and impairing customer service!

Here are ways to be supportive:

> *Be respectful rather than attacking the person. Start by asking the question, "Are you aware...?" (For example, "Are you aware of the effect your mood is having on others?")*

> *Ask if you can do or say something that will help them get a better perspective or to feel happy to be at work. If the offer is declined, let the person know that you expect them to shift focus and become a team player.*

> *In other words, be compassionate by not allowing the person to be stuck in misery, but also don't permit the condition to become contagious.*

It's your day and your life. Don't get sucked into negativity.

What Really Is Your Job?

What is your job? Your job description lists your duties and areas for which you specifically will be held accountable. But that doesn't really answer the question completely. You can do everything in the job description and still not get the job done.

Regardless of job title and official duties, first and foremost your job is to take care of the patients! Maybe sterilizing instruments is not in your job description; but help out if the sterilization tech is falling behind. If you have a few minutes to spare and your front desk team is backed up with patients and phone calls, *help out!* If you have spare time, resist checking your cell phone—instead engage the patient in conversation.

This is what real teamwork looks like: not just getting your own job done but also making sure that everyone else is supported in getting *their* job done. It all adds up to putting the patient first! And this is what job security looks like as well! The better the experience of service for the patient, the more referrals they will generate. They win—the practice wins—you win!

6

Goal Setting

The world wasn't formed in a day, and neither were we. Set small goals and build upon them.—Lee Haney

The Clock is Ticking

While we can measure time down to fractions of a second or up to grand epochs and eons, the only real measurement that counts for us is the experience of time and how we relate to it. For a patient waiting fifteen minutes to be seen, it may seem like an hour, but for the clinician who doesn't know how to catch up, time seems to fly by.

Time is an irreplaceable asset. If you lose a dollar, you can get another dollar. If you waste a minute, it's gone forever. And therein lies the rub. Too many of us spend our irretrievable time in the present complaining about, mourning, criticizing, blaming, and wishing for the past. We don't seem to recognize that we are wasting the moment in present time.

There is, however, an exception to this. When you look at past events for the purpose of learning what to do or not to do in the future, then that is time well spent. It is particularly effective when you take the viewpoint that you are responsible for all your experiences. You can't control the circumstances, but you can choose your responses to them.

Review your past year by noting what worked and what didn't work for you during the year. Then ask yourself what lessons you can learn from those experiences that will support you in attaining your goals in the new twelve months. Make a "clean slate" upon which you set your goals. Create each year as a building block to achieving your dreams. Don't drag the past into the present and then wonder why things never change.

Never be a prisoner of your past. It was just a lesson, not a life sentence.—unknown

What Are You Waiting For?

About half my lifetime ago, I participated in a ropes course in the Berkshire Mountains. The first of three courses was a zip line about a thousand feet over a canyon. I stood on the outcropping boulder, tightly gripping the T-bar high above my head, looking down at the trees and rocks *way* down below. This could be the end of my life—what was I thinking when I signed up to do this?!

Cognitively, I realized, of course, I was strapped into a safety harness that the course leaders had assured us could hold an elephant without breaking. I was still skeptical—could this rope and harness actually hold my body for the five-hundred-foot run across the canyon? As I stood on the precipice I panicked, screaming at the course leader that I wasn't ready, that I needed different gloves, that the harness wasn't on right, and any other thing I could think of to get out of this situation. No such luck. The course rules were that you would go on your own time, and that no one would force you, but there was no mention of quitting! The tension of the zip line was such that when I grabbed the T-bar, it hoisted me up on my tip toes and I couldn't pull it down further. In my attempt to get a more stable footing on the rock, I unwittingly ended up tip-toeing my way off the ledge.

To this day, I still recall vividly the sensation of flying across the canyon with an indescribable sense of freedom and joy. When I landed on the other side, I felt ecstatic, and I knew something had forever changed in me. I knew if I could step off that ledge despite feeling nearly paralyzed by fear, I could handle whatever other doubts that I wasn't ready or good enough to pursue my dreams. Within a year, I had launched my speaking career.

When we look at our personal heroes, or anyone whom we want to emulate, we see the end result, not the process. We make assumptions about their "overnight successes" and don't see the personal struggles they had to overcome in order to succeed. We compare ourselves to the "end result" and then believe we're not ready or not good enough.

All of us reach precipices in life, when self-doubt roars in our heads, telling us we're not ready to be a parent, go to college, get a promotion, sing in the choir, run a 10K, lose weight, or make a difference in someone's life. I say, "Go to the roar!"

It's your life! The time is now! Take a leap of faith! Ecstasy awaits. Ready-Set-GO!

> *You don't have to be great to get started, but you have to get started to be great.*—Les Brown

Where Did The Excitement Go?

In 2016, The American Association of Orthodontists annual meeting just took place in Orlando, FL. The four days were crammed with great speakers in both orthodontic techniques and every aspect of practice management, including many inspirational speakers on personal development, leadership, and customer service. I could just feel the energy among the attendees, and I heard many conversations of what changes they would enact when they got back home.

So many great intentions! And then something happens. We go home from the meeting and get back into "the swing of things," but in a very short period of time, it's "business as usual" and the meeting becomes merely a fond memory.

What can you do to sustain the excitement and institute real change? Before attending the next conference, consider the meeting's agenda, then collaborate with your team to consider what areas of the practice you would like to refresh and enhance. Decide who among you will attend which specific lectures. Have another meeting as soon after the convention as possible and have attendees give reports on what benefits they derived. During this meeting, create specific plans of action to implement the ideas and decide who will be in charge of these actions.

The bigger challenge will be how to sustain excitement and inspiration from the meetings, especially when not everyone on the team attended. It's important to engage those who could not attend. When sharing, bring up points of interest for *everyone,* and avoid "insider jokes" that will make some feel puzzled or left out of the conversations. Most important, at every morning huddle, share one thing that inspired or motivated you, and plan on how to make that come alive in the practice that day.

Morning huddle

Inspiration and motivation don't last when left unattended. To quote the father of motivational speakers, Zig Ziglar: "People often say that motivation doesn't last. Well, neither does bathing, that's why we recommend it daily." It's up to you to keep the flames of passion and purpose burning brightly!

Satisfaction Guaranteed Isn't Enough!

It's somewhat amusing to me how many ads scream *Satisfaction guaranteed!* Even more surprising is how many consumers seem impressed by the promise that "we will meet your minimum expectations!" The message also implies, "we will perform the same as our competitors."

Patients or customers want more than satisfaction—they *expect* to be satisfied or they wouldn't come to you to in the first place. This is especially true when people are buying big ticket items—things or services they have planned or saved for. Getting braces (or crowns, veneers or dental implants, etc.) takes a big commitment on the patient's part. People want more than mere satisfaction, they want empathy, compassion, and service that match the commitment and effort they have made. When they "shop" for a provider, they are not looking for satisfaction; they want to be *appreciated and assured* that they are making the right choice.

While verbal expressions of appreciation and assurance are valuable, people rely more on their experience of what they see and whether they feel special. If what you say doesn't match their experience, they won't believe you, and they certainly won't feel in sync with you.

It doesn't take much to make patients feel welcome. A genuine smile and greeting, eye contact, and showing interest in them and their interests go way beyond the mere collection of their medical history. It is critical that the emotional atmosphere of the practice be happy and upbeat. New patients will immediately assess whether team members are friendly with each other and with other patients. Everyone in the reception area must seem comfortable and at ease—as if they are in a really nice place!

These are the basics if you want to match prospective patients' expectations. When you have the basics down, you can then ask yourself, "What can I do to *exceed* their expectations?" Ask that every day in your morning huddle as a way to focus the team, and you will blow the competition away!

Who's The Boss?

For an employee, the answer to this question seems easy: *Whoever signs my paycheck!* For an employer, though, the answer is more complicated.

I'm my own boss! you might think. Examine the evidence, though. As the employer, your decisions about the direction of your company and the actions you take are shaped by your prior successes, the amount of discretionary funds available, the current economic climate, and certainly the expertise of

Goal Setting

your team, among other things. At times you may feel dominated by all these situations that seem to restrict your freedom, but the bottom line is that you choose the path you are on and the consequences that come with that choice.

There is a deeper and more meaningful examination of the "who's the boss" question that allows for freedom even in the face of restrictions. In fact, you really *are* the "boss," the *chooser* in your life, whether you recognize it or not. It is easy to forget this as life is rushing at us, and sometimes we make choices based solely on what we want at that moment. We react to and satisfy urges and feelings rather than make choices based on long-term commitments.

For example, you decide to go on a diet, but a week or so into it, you "cave in" and eat a pint of ice cream! You love your kids and your spouse, but you've had a hectic day, you're tired and your patience is worn thin, and suddenly you snap at them unnecessarily. You love your job and the people you work with, but when someone doesn't perform up to standards or behaves poorly in some way, you avoid a confrontation, instead complaining to anyone who will listen. At these moments, you have made your *feelings* your boss.

If you really want what you say you want—peace, prosperity, happiness, health, love and great relationships—then you have to stay focused on the long-term, end result, and not let your feelings rule the roost! Complaining to others instead of communicating to the person directly doesn't take the problem away. Similarly, eating the ice cream reinforces the "I can't do this" conversation and weakens your resolve; snapping at your spouse or children doesn't bring them closer to you but rather creates tension or even fear.

The "muscle" of intention needs to be exercised daily or it will atrophy. The more you choose to stay true to your commitments rather than give in to your feelings, the more you exercise the intention muscle, the stronger it gets; and you take another step toward your goal!

Are We There Yet?

In Fourteen-hundred, ninety-two, Columbus sailed the ocean blue was the start of a ditty most of us recited in school as a way of learning history. There were so many dates, locations, facts, and names of famous people! But what was often left out was overwhelming struggle of the historical journeys.

Most adults recall long car trips, when *Are we there yet?* rolled off of our tongues endlessly. Numerous car games were invented by adults, perhaps to distract the kids but also to gain some relief for the adults! Nowadays, technology has come to the rescue, and kids can be silenced and distracted with video games, movies, and music.

Consider that most of our road trips don't last more than a few hours; Columbus sailed for months! Instead of *Are we there yet?* his growingly mutinous crew probably complained *Are we ever going to get there!*

Historic events, such as Columbus' "discovering" of America, can serve as lessons in human growth— opportunities for deepening compassion and perspective. Similarly, when I am working with a client, I have to remind them where we started and how far we've come, because unlike the family road trip, there is no actual destination. We have heard, *Excellence is a journey, not a destination,* yet we need to know how far along the journey we have come. Reminding ourselves, and our clients, how far we have come validates the length of the journey. But we must also keep attuned to the more subtle indicators of success, such as an easing of stress, an upbeat attitude on Monday morning, a rejuvenated sense of purpose, and poise in the face of breakdowns and upsets.

> *Success is a journey, not a destination. The doing is often more important than the outcome.*—**Arthur Ashe**

7

Relationships

Caring about the other person's emotional state is the most powerful and authentic way for you to create long-term, loyal relationships; both personally and professionally.—Ross Shafer

Faults and Forgiveness

One man's trash is another man's treasure is an old adage that has application broader than as a mere guide to yard sale shopping. In fact, it's in the *labeling* of "trash" or "treasure" that determines the value of something, rather than the thing itself. In other words, *beauty lies in the eye of the beholder,* another wise adage that points to the power the speaker has, realized or not.

Therein lies the rub. While you may think someone is an idiot, another might think that person is brilliant. You find someone unattractive, someone else finds them beautiful. You detest even being near someone, but another yearns to be with that person.

In cases such as these, no one is right and no one is wrong! You are not hired to like everyone, you were hired to collaborate, cooperate, and get along as a team to produce the best result in the most efficient way possible. In the same way, you also don't get to choose which patients you like or dislike and then treat them accordingly. If you are an employee, your boss chooses with whom to do business and your job is to provide service at the level promised.

With that being said, I don't mean to imply that you should accept, tolerate or endorse anyone being disrespectful, domineering, or abusive towards others. People who are that negative probably comprise *less than* 10% of all the people with whom you come in contact. When there is a "personality clash" between you and a coworker, remember that your nemesis is having as much difficulty getting along with you as you are with them. They see your faults easier than they see your gifts, and they get as annoyed with you as you do with them. It's like looking in a weird mirror that reflects your feelings rather than your image.

You want to be seen in your best light and to have your faults and shortcomings overlooked or forgiven. And so do they. Now, you can wait for the other person to step up and forgive first, but I believe the world needs fewer spectators and more heroes who are willing to take the risk and "save the day." What is actually at risk is ego and what is at stake is peace, harmony, and workability. As Dr. Phil (McGraw) often says, "You can be right or you can be happy!"

The first step in creating more work-ability is to forgive as you want to be forgiven, and to view the other person through the eyes of that person's loved ones rather than your own. The second step is to have a facilitated communication meeting in which both of you make respectful requests of each other. For instance:

I request that when you want me to do something that takes me away from what I am working on, you first ask me if I have the time to talk, and then make a request rather than give me an order.

No one is perfect. We all have assets and faults. Look for and speak to the highest in each other and forgive the rest!

Confronting Confrontation

One of the more common breakdowns in relationships is avoiding confrontation. I say it's a *breakdown* because avoiding handling a bothersome or troubling situation between two or more people not only fails to resolve the issue, but it also starts to create little mine fields around the relationship, as in *Don't go there!*

The primary reason for this behavior is we fear the loss of the relationship if we speak up about the problem, so we decide the issue isn't worth the risk. This is quite understandable, but the cost of this choice can be high— erosion of trust, loss of affinity, pent-up emotions, negative judgments, etc. I am not claiming that we should go about *confronting people* with issues. I am just as uncomfortable with this notion as anyone else. Instead, I favor *confronting issues* with people. If you confront *people*, you will get a defensive response that can spiral into an argument and finger-pointing. However, if you confront issues *with* people, you create partnering with them—resolve the problems and blame no one.

This latter approach is rooted in two beliefs: First, when a problem arises, look initially at the system as the source of the breakdown. Second, people are doing the best they can with what they have to work with, and when they have better tools or know better, they perform better. The approach may look like this:

> **Person A:** *I've noticed a problem that I would like to address with you so that we can come up with a solution that works for everyone. Would you be willing to do that?*

> **Person B:** *Sure...what's the problem?*

> **Person A:** *When we are running behind schedule, and we get stressed out, we seem to be abrupt and impatient with each other. I know this is not intentional, and yet it seems to add to the stress. What do you think we can do to be more supportive of each other when we are stressed?*

If Person B doesn't have any suggestions, then it is up to Person A to offer one. The axiom at work here: If you have a problem, don't just complain about it, offer a solution. This is the starting point for negotiating a resolution that works for all concerned. Please note that nowhere in the above conversation is anyone blamed for the problem or made to feel wrong. It also presumes a relationship of cooperation that promotes teamwork and collaboration.

This form of confrontation might feel awkward at first, but remember, all new exercises or skills feel uncomfortable in the beginning phases—with practice, it gets easier. The best part of this is it requires you to be conscious in your speaking, and that's always a good thing. It also maintains a sense of dignity and respect for all concerned.

Heroes Needed!

Perhaps the most significant issue that motivates a doctor to bring me in for a consult is gossip. The originating request is typically to improve teamwork and communication, but the root of the problem is gossip.

I define gossip as a complaint that a person has about someone but takes it to someone else who can do nothing about it. For instance, if Jane has a problem with Mary, instead of talking to Mary about it, she tells Suzie. All Suzie can do is commiserate with Jane, and most likely Suzie will then tell someone else about Jane's problem with Mary. In a short time, people take sides about who's right and who's wrong, and all of it is spoken in whispers or behind closed doors. The end result is a divided team, and the original problem is still in place.

When I work with a team to resolve their "personality conflicts," the greatest obstacle to creating the peace and harmony that everyone is actually yearning for is the lack of forgiveness. If you are unwilling to let go of the offense, even when the issue is addressed in a respectful and compassionate manner, nothing good can be accomplished. What is wanted and needed is someone to be the hero—to accept an apology, to forgive and let go, to focus on a higher purpose and intent. You don't need to like each other, but you do need to respect each other. We all have a different perspective on life, sourced from different histories and circumstances that mold and shape us. Forgiveness frees all involved and allows for the possibility of harmony and peace.

Be the hero and everyone will be happy!

Live in such a way that you would not be ashamed to sell your parrot to the town gossip.—Will Rogers

Label Tools

Tools are neither good nor bad, they just *are.* How we use them determines their usefulness. For instance, a hammer is an important tool in construction projects but it can also be used to hurt or maim someone. The person holding the hammer determines its use, whether for good or bad.

The same can be said about labels. They are very useful in sorting information and in identifying objects, projects, and items needing to be categorized for easy recognition. I even have a label making printer that I use to print the titles of my client folders and projects so I can store and retrieve information on them easily.

Labels are also very useful in creating foundations of mutual understanding. For example, when doctors refer to "Class 1" or "Class 2" occlusion, other doctors and related professionals will immediately recognize the reference and understand the related issues. This allows for a common ground in ensuing conversations without having to explain the meaning of the label, as would be necessary for a layperson.

However, we tend to become lazy when using labels, in that we operate as if the label tells us everything we need to know about the subject. I've heard doctors and teams refer to a person as a Class 2, rather than the person *having* a Class 2 occlusion. We then act as if we know all that we need to know about him or her. With regard to treatment or protocol, this may be true, but if that becomes the basis for relating to that person, then there is no real relationship happening. People *have* symptoms, but they are not *the* symptom. People *have* problems, but they are not *the* problem. Instead of labeling a person as "autistic," consider instead that they are a person who *has* autism.

Labels used negatively or without thought often cause relationships to sour or even prevent them from developing at all. Remember, labels are tools; how you use them determines their usefulness.

8

Work Ethic:
Growing the Business

The very striving and hard work that we so constantly try to avoid is the major building block in the person we are today—**Pope Paul VI**

Petri Dish Formula for Success

Do you remember biology classes where you were taught how to grow bacteria? First determine what kind of bacteria you want to grow, then put their favorite food in a dish, provide the right amount of heat and light, and in time, *voila!*, you have masses of bacteria evident in the petri dish.

For any business to succeed and grow, it must cultivate a convincing message and project it to current and future clients. That is the purpose of having a website, Facebook page, or other social media accounts—to communicate to the population at large that you are open for business! The question that business owners need to ask is: *With whom do I want to do business?"*

The answer cannot be "anyone" or "everyone," because you cannot please "everyone," and "anyone" can end up being a real disruption to your success. It's important, therefore, to clearly define yourself and who you want as your patient. Then design your practice around attracting and pleasing that type of patient. For instance, if you want to attract "high-end" patients, the interior design of your office needs to be "high-end" and fashionable. If you want more adults in your practice, chances are you will not use the "open bay" arrangement but rather have privacy walls for each chair.

Work Ethic

When you know who your "perfect" patient is, you will also know whom to please and whose opinion counts. From time to time, a client will tell me about a problem with a patient (or often a patient's parent) and will ask me how to handle the situation. The answer depends on how close a match that person is to the characteristics and attributes of the "perfect" patient. The patient or parent may be very demanding or non-compliant, yet blame the doctor or assistant for the lack of progress. Often there is an associated delinquency in appointments or payments. The simple question becomes: *Why try to please someone who cannot be pleased or doesn't appreciate being pleased?* You may hesitate to dismiss a patient because you fear what they may say about you—if so, you are being "held hostage."

I don't often recommend dismissing a patient, but when I do, I coach the doctor to do it in such a way that the patient is not unhappy or angry. The best part is the relief the team experiences, and on a more subtle level, the improvement it makes to team attitude and office atmosphere.

Whether you own a dental practice or a small business, the more clarity you have about the values, characteristics, and attributes you commit to, the easier it will be to create an environment that naturally attracts people who share your view and want to help you grow.

The Gift of Work

Henry Giles, a Unitarian minister and writer (1809-1892) said this about work:

> *Man must work, that is certain as the sun. But he may work grudgingly or he may work gratefully; he may work as a man or he may work as a machine. There is no work so rude, that he may not exalt it; no work so impassive, that he may not breathe a soul into it; no work so dull that he may not enliven it.*

It speaks to a natural human desire for people to want to know that they *matter*—that they are contributing and participating fully in life. Because most adults spend the majority of their waking hours at work, the ideal situation is for people to have the experience that their work matters and that they are appreciated for what they do, regardless of the nature of the job!

Giles' statement refers to *any* work, whether it's life-saving surgery or collecting trash. The important factor to note is that it is the person who exalts the work, breathes a soul into it and enlivens it, not the other way around. Furthermore, it's choice!

I vividly recall an interaction I had many years ago with a women's bathroom attendant in a busy airport. I was so impressed with her cheerful and energetic attitude as she cleaned the toilet stalls that I engaged her in conversation, asking her how she maintained such a positive demeanor doing what most of us would consider to be menial work. Her answer was brilliant: "Anytime I don't like what I'm doing, that's the Devil tempting me!" She had created a powerful context around her work that enabled her to maintain a state of joy. Then she asked me how I would rate her work. I said it was excellent. She then asked me, "Don't you want someplace to come where you could do what you need to do without worrying about where you're doing it?" I replied, "Of course!" And her final statement to me was, "Well then, I got my job done and I count too, don't I!"

Life is a mirror that reflects back whatever you bring to it! If you want to feel satisfied and fulfilled in your work, show up already satisfied! Start your day being grateful you have meaningful work that contributes to others' well-being and happiness. If you think you have to be the head honcho in order to matter, just think about how limited your doctor or boss would be without each person playing their part in "getting the job done!" You count if you say so! You "breathe life" into your work. You rule!

Work Ethic

When we do the best we can, we never know what miracle is wrought in our life, or in the life of another.—Helen Keller

Keep the Pedal to the Metal

I often hear from a prospective client when their practice is in some kind of crisis: new patient call-ins are way down, production and collections are down, there's tension among team members and the doctor—coming to work is just not fun anymore. In the interview process with the client, it becomes evident that the situation didn't "just happen" but rather began months before and went unnoticed until it could no longer be ignored.

More often than not, the problem can be traced back to the erroneous assumption that something that is working will continue to work once the structure or system is in place. What the assumption does not take into consideration is that everything is subject to the *law of entropy*. This complex law can be more easily understood as explained by Tega Jessa, contributor to Universe Today:

> *The natural tendency of the universe is to fall apart into disorder. A well-known illustration is the messy room concept. You know that you need to constantly work at keeping your room clean and well arranged. However, you know that if you don't keep up with the routine the room will gradually return to its messy state.*

This is true even in personal relationships. "The honeymoon is over" occurs when the couple stops injecting romance into the relationship and makes assumptions that "now that we are married, I shouldn't have to _____ (fill in the blank)."

Relationships, whether at work or personal, deteriorate when communications are withheld until tempers flare. Systems that are put in place and then presumed to run on their own begin to deteriorate. The only thing that intervenes with entropy is a conscious being: the person who keeps the room clean; the one who keeps romance alive; the person who doesn't let "petty" grievances turn into major problems; the doctor who follows up and ensures that the systems in place are working as planned.

> *Another flaw in the human character is that everybody wants to build and nobody wants to do maintenance.*—Kurt Vonnegut

Mise en Place!

Once I was speaking with my friend Paul, a masterful professional chef who also teaches at a culinary institute, and he told me about *mise en place.* It is the very first thing he learned as a culinary student and now teaches to his students. The French phrase (pronounced "mi zã 'plas") means "putting in place," and for chefs, refers to organizing and arranging all the ingredients and tools needed for the meals to be prepared during a shift. Paul said you can't afford to waste time looking for an ingredient or special knife, etc., once you start cooking and are expected to get meals out to the customers on time.

While he was talking, I heard my mother's voice in my head nagging us as kids to "put things back where you found them" so we would know where things were when we needed them. *A place for everything and everything in its place.* Similarly, she had us set out our clothes the night before a school day so we wouldn't waste time getting dressed in the morning. It's how she managed to get five kids to school on time and my dad to the train station for his 7:00 a.m. trip to the city!

Paul also remarked how mise en place is important in any business; everything has to be "in place" before doors open for business. In a dental practice, these questions should be asked: Are all the stations in the operatories fully stocked with the hand pieces, brackets, and tools needed that day? Is the coffee machine in the reception area stocked with coffee and accoutrements? Are the magazines and games for the kids in place? Are the files for the scheduled patients readily available? Are the operatories, consult rooms, and reception area clean and neat and ready for patients? When the team arrives for work, are makeup and hair already done, breakfast already eaten? Or do people "slide in under the wire" a minute before the morning huddle, and eat breakfast, finish applying makeup during the meeting, and then rush out to the operatories to stock the chairs? Is everything "in its place," or do you and the team waste time searching for an instrument or bracket?

Paul said when things start to get harried in the kitchen and meals are being delayed, he admonishes his students to "mise your station!" While that may appear at first to delay things even more, he said the time lost at that moment will be made up in the next.

So "mise your practice" before the first patient or customer walks in!

Persistence Pays!

Here is a confession: Almost every week, when I struggled for a topic for week's message, I frequently asked myself, *What were you thinking?!* when I decided back in 2012 to write a weekly message.

Every week, as the deadline approached, I started racking my brain for something to say that would be useful, meaningful, interesting, and supportive for my readers. Every week I would do battle with the little voice in my head that came up with a plethora of excuses and justifications for skipping a week or two.

What motivated me to plow through the "I don't wanna" is my belief that it's more important to have the results in life than the reasons why I don't have them. Reasons for not having results are easy, but I don't want to be an expert in excuses; I'd rather exercise and build up my "can do" muscles. In the total scheme of things, the Monday Morning

Message doesn't rate in the top 100 "what's important in life" list, but keeping my word does!

The choices we make in life always have a payoff. Keeping your word leads to a sense of accomplishment, satisfaction, and stronger self-esteem. Not keeping your word leads to a sense of weakness, loss of pride, and decreased self-worth. Honoring your word in the "little" things pays off in the long run when you encounter situations that are the "big" things in your life.

Persistence pays handsomely! Keep on keeping on with the little things and the big things will come easier!

WIIFM

All of us are always (and mostly unconsciously) tuned into an internal radio station WIIFM, the *What's In It For Me* station! While at first glance this may sound selfish, it is really quite a useful way to evaluate a situation that helps us make choices in life. If we eliminate any judgments about this human trait, whether it's good or bad, right or wrong, or selfish or not, we can use it to attain our goals, especially when they involve others' support or agreement.

For example, almost every practice conducts an office tour as part of the new patient's orientation to the practice. Unfortunately, too often this tour is conducted in a rote manner without considering the patient's point of view. As a case in point, when I went for an initial exam at a dentist's office, one of the team members took me on a tour of the office. For me, it was a boring experience and a "time filler" without much purpose to it. It was as though the staff member had been told to do this by a consultant to the practice or a speaker at a meeting they attended. The tour seemed so mundane to me: "Here is the reception area, these are the operatory and consult rooms, here we sterilize." What I got was a checklist, not an orientation.

The tour could have gone like this: "Welcome to our practice! I'd like to show you around and introduce you to some of our team members so you can feel at home here. I know you met Ginny when you checked in; each time you come, you can sign in here and we will make sure we have all your information and materials ready. This is our sterilization area, which is maintained to a hospital standard." There would be much more, of course, but the idea is to focus on the client—let them know "what's in it for them" to be a part of your practice.

Old Enough To Be New

My maternal grandfather was a very successful designer of women's coats and suits. He had a saying that was popular in the fashion industry: *Old enough to be new.* Just a minor change and a new name, and *voila!,* a new fashion trend was discovered. Bell bottom pants became Palazzo pants, which became boot cut pants, and so on. The long straight skirts stylish for women in the early 1900s kept evolving the hem line, and suddenly the "pencil" skirt became the fashion. What's old to some is brand new to younger people who weren't around when a certain style was all the rage.

This principle can be particularly useful from a marketing standpoint. To be effective, marketing activities distinguish a business from its competitors in memorable ways. Since the modern and most popular way to communicate with people is either through texting or email, snail mail has become a mark of distinction and is especially impactful when sending "we care" messages of praise, congratulations or support to patients. Perhaps you had a really fun game for patients years ago, such as the "Pick Your Nose" contest—you make alginate models of the doctor's noses, and patients have to identify whose nose is whose. The patients who played that game have cycled out of the practice and you now have a whole new population of patients who never saw or heard of the game.

The point is, "old" is rich in ideas for new and exciting. Don't just discard the past. Look for the gems there that can be polished up and used to brighten the present.

Practice Ambassadors

Every practice has, or should have, a policy manual that includes job descriptions and titles for each department and for the team as a whole. The number one job description for everyone is Practice Ambassador! Among the definitions of "ambassador" found in the dictionary is: "an authorized representative or messenger." The application here is that every member of the team is an ambassador. Representing the practice supersedes actual duties of any job.

A friend of mine told me of recently visiting his dentist for a cleaning. He was sheepish in admitting it had been three years since his last appointment. "When I finally got the courage to make an appointment, I got there only to find out the practice had been sold to another dentist," he related. This really didn't bother him and he went through with his appointment with the new hygienist, who not only was rough with him, but repeatedly commented on how he really needed to be coming in more often to avoid the tartar build up, and so on. He went on:

> *I already knew! It took courage and humility to even show up again. I had no pain, no immediate emergency to be there. I would have much rather have heard someone say, "I notice you have not been here for a while. I will try to be as gentle as I can, but know that there is a buildup I have to take care of. Please be patient and let me know if there is too much pain.*

My friend concluded his story:

> *Just knowing I was cared for and that someone realized my situation would have made the experience much better. I did not feel valued so much as judged.*

*And I had judged myself enough already. I still will go
back, but wonder if I should say something or not.
She had a point about my need to be a regular visitor,
yet I felt like I was being punished for showing up.*

Yes, the hygienist got her job done insofar as cleaning my
friend's teeth, but as an ambassador, she conveyed a
negative message for the practice. She also missed the
opportunity to create a fan for the new dentist and a patient
who looked forward to being there again.

In your commitment to get the "doingness" of your job
done well, make sure you don't forget that your primary job
is being an ambassador whose mission it is to create friends
and fans of the practice.

Why You?

Most dental and orthodontic websites have a link titled
"What Sets Us Apart." That is indeed a good thing to
promote so that visitors to your site can, hopefully,
distinguish your practice from your competitors. If everyone
is claiming the same "distinction," however, then
prospective patients don't have much on which to base their
judgments. It would be prudent to check out what others
are saying about their own practices so you can make sure
you stand out.

Perhaps the most important distinction to make is one
that will educate patients in making an informed choice: the
difference between straight teeth and a beautiful smile, and
between seeing a professional and a "DIY" online or mail-in
order. There are so many TV and print ads promising to
straighten teeth without having to go to an orthodontist,
and for a fraction of what an orthodontist will charge. In one
ad, the actor/patient touts that you can "bypass the
middleman." (Did you know you are just a "middleman"?!)
The main distinction in these ads is price; it's certainly not
quality of treatment or even good dental health that is long-

lasting. You know that, of course, but does the potential patient visitor to your website?

More than ever before, people need to be informed about orthodontics and the differences among the options they now have. In addition to being "user friendly," your website and social media sites need to engage people so they can understand the differences in treatment options. Patient reviews and testimonials, both written and on video, can validate the benefits of being treated by professionals and the advantage of a great service experience. When potential patients come to your office, they need to feel that it was well worth the trip, instead of merely avoiding the middle man! They should also want to be a part of your "family" and have fun while being treated.

Orthodontics has always involved change and will continue to do so in the future. The private practitioner can and will thrive if they embrace rather resist change. Stay focused on what sets you apart!

The Problem with Experience

John Borrowman and I have been friends for close to 35 years. He is a recruiter for a specialized area in the financial sector called "business valuation." While our businesses are very different from one another, there are common grounds that intersect in the areas of relationships and management issues. We enjoy sharing our newsletters with each other.

In conversations I've had with clients, a recurring theme has been how to deal with "senior" staff who resist training new team members. Their range of complaints includes: *It's too tiring; They're not a good fit so why put in the effort when they're going to leave; They don't have a good work ethic*; and *I have enough to do just getting my own job done.*

I have to remind people that when they first started out in their careers, *they* were the novices—they didn't even know what they didn't know! Because someone else took the time to train them, they moved up the scale of learning to become proficient and even expert in their jobs. I ask them where they would be today had their "superiors" taken the same position and were impatient or "too tired" to train them.

In a recent newsletter, John Borrowman addressed the same issue from another angle and in a thoughtful and insightful way. With his permission I share these excerpts.

The Problem With Experience

You wouldn't think that experience could be a problem. But when you've known what you know for so long that you've forgotten what it's like not to know it, that can be a problem.

It can be a problem when it comes to developing younger, more purpose-driven staff. They want to learn and grow, and they need your guidance. Giving them that guidance requires you to think differently about their learning. For one thing, it will happen differently from what you went through. Much of that difference is generational.

Your younger staffers are not looking for a hand-out, but they are looking for a hand up. And that's not necessarily the "check-list" you might think it is. Sometimes it can seem like they expect to be handed the roadmap to guaranteed success when, in fact, all they want is to know what forward progress looks like and how to measure it.

The more you know, the harder it is to remember what you had to learn to get where you are. Couple that with changes in the way young staff learn and grow, and you can't afford *not* to think differently.

The One

In a recent conversation with a coaching client, the doctor told me he had overheard one of his clinical assistants telling another assistant that she wouldn't refer her friends to his practice for treatment. She said this while standing near the operatory. Hopefully none of the patients and parents were in ear-shot. At the end of the day, the doctor met with the assistant and asked her why she had said that. Rather than answer his question, she quit in a very dramatic fashion.

What became apparent was that the woman's heart was not in her work, or at least not in her work at that practice. Sometimes we humans give up looking for "The One" and settle for "The One for Now," or "The Better Than No One." It almost always ends in failure, whether it's a job or a relationship. When we make choices out of desperation, at some point in time we find ourselves in a worse mess than if we had just waited it out and continued the search.

This often happens when a practice is short-staffed and desperate for a trained team member, and the doctor decides having someone on the job is better than no one. Often the new hire never quite matches expectations, is constantly corrected, and either gets fired, quits, or worse yet, stays but is unhappy. It works the same way for the person who is looking for a job but settles for something less than desired. Sometimes, unfortunately, termination cannot be avoided, and when it comes to parting ways, there's always a price to pay for everyone—emotionally, time-wise, and financially.

So how do you find The One? The first step is to be clear about what you must have and must not have in a team member, and what you should or should not have. The "should" section indicates what is negotiable—nice to have but not deal-breakers. Understand that the "must have" and "must not have" are deal-breakers. If you accept someone or a job that doesn't fit the bill, you need to be responsible for breaking your own standards and not make the other person wrong for the choice you made.

Work Ethic

When someone is hired for a job, the fundamental agreement for the hire is to support the mission of the business and help it grow. When an owner hires someone, the fundamental agreement is to support that person in being successful in the job. Those agreements become more difficult to keep with "The One For Now."

Finally, if you do hire someone or if you accept a job out of necessity, keep the unspoken agreement to perform as if you have found The One.

I Know, I Know!

Most of our lives are spent in learning something. By the time we enter kindergarten we have already learned how to speak, walk, and manipulate our environment, and today's kids have also learned how to use tablets and smart phones. We spend twelve or more years in formal education, then many more hours getting trained in specific job tasks.

For many people, being "in the know" is critically important. They seem to know everything about everything and try to impress others with their encyclopedic range of information.

But is knowing really all it's cracked up to be? This type of knowing can actually be a barrier to learning. When we resort to the "I already know" position, it shuts down exploration, investigation, curiosity, and even collaboration. In effect, it guarantees the status quo and stifles progress.

Being able to say "I don't know" doesn't mean you're stupid; if fact, it may even be a sign of confidence and an indication of a willingness to learn. Granted, there are some people who are stuck in their own insecurities and when they hear you admit you don't know something, they might think less of you. Remember, that is *their* problem, not yours. Being open to learning is a valuable asset, especially in this rapidly expanding information age, and it will keep you young at heart!

It Has Sprung!

It's always such a wonderful experience when spring finally arrives in a colorful array of colors splashing the landscape, from the trees budding, lawns greening, and daffodils and tulips erupting. It does tend to lighten one's mood and put a bounce in one's step, even if for just a few moments. Whether or not you celebrate Easter or Passover or the Rites of Spring, humans have for millennia looked to spring as a season of hope and rebirth.

What we see flourish in the spring are the seeds we had planted months before. I plant daffodils, tulips and hyacinths in November and watch their collective beauty bloom in the spring. The clients and engagements I have now are the result of conversations that took place months ago.

Similarly, the patients you see today didn't just show up out of nowhere. They are the result of the "seeds" you planted either intentionally, accidentally, or even indirectly through patient or doctor referrals. Just as my flowers were the result of intentional plantings, marketing is an intentional action that requires planning.

While active marketing requires specific plans of action ("Share a Smile" cards for patient referrals, lunches for referring doctors, "muffin runs," etc.), there also is the more indirect aspect of marketing—the emotional atmosphere of the practice. My bulbs bloomed because they were in fertile soil; they would not fare so well in arid sand. Your active marketing plans will not yield the desired results if the patients are not "wowed" by the experience of being with you.

The "fertile soil" for your marketing requires a team that is happy and grateful for the work they do. It is crucial that they appreciate each other and the doctor and are focused on making each patient's visit one in which they feel glad to be there.

Work Ethic

In order to keep my garden blooming, I have to fertilize and water the soil, plus pull weeds as needed. To keep your workplace thriving, "weed" out gossip, be quick to praise, have an attitude of gratitude, and have corrective conversations that foster learning while maintaining respect and dignity for each other.

Judge each day not by the harvest you reap but by the seeds that you plant.—**Robert Louis Stevenson**

Expectations

We have all seen a bumper sticker, magnet, or poster that shouts, *Expect a Miracle!* I understand the philosophy behind that and the encouragement it is meant to impart. I myself set my sights high and believe the best is yet to come. The pessimist's point of view is that lower expectations protect us from disappointments.

What about expectations? I once heard a seminar leader define "expectation" as an upset waiting to happen. This is also true. One idea does not invalidate the other if you understand the power behind both notions. The first is meant to support optimism and a positive outlook on life, and the other is meant to manage emotional states. Expectations do have a "hook" inherent in them: When we don't get what we expect, we not only feel upset, but we also feel that some "right" has been violated—we expected it, so it should have happened, so now we've been wronged!

Logic tells us that this kind of reaction is silly. If we understand both sides of this "coin" called expectations, we can use it to our advantage. Manage expectations—yours and those of others. In business, you manage your patients' expectations when you implicitly under-promise but then over-deliver. Your patient's expectations are far exceeded! Tell a patient that a procedure will take thirty minutes, and they are delighted when it is done in only twenty-five.

Expect a miracle, and manage reality!

9
Problem Solving

If we had no winter, the spring would not be so pleasant; if we did not sometimes taste of adversity, prosperity would not be so welcome.— **Anne Bradstreet**

TGFP!

Thank Goodness for Problems! No, I'm not crazy and I'm not wishing ill on anybody, but let's face it: If it weren't for problems, you wouldn't have a job!

If everyone had a spacious, well-constructed, safe home, there would be no need for contractors and builders. If everyone were in perfect health, there would be no need for doctors, nurses, hospitals and support staff. If we didn't need to eat, there would be no farmers, grocery stores, or restaurants. And if everyone had perfect teeth? You guessed it, orthodontists and dentists would have no profession!

Problems have also inspired genius! Polio moved Jonas Salk to discover and develop a vaccine for polio. The inability to widely disperse knowledge led to the Gutenberg moveable type printing press (c. 1439). The first programmable computer dates back to 1936, but it was Bill Gates in the 1980s had the vision of bringing desktop computers to every home. What followed was the rapid growth of personal computers and innumerable break-throughs in technology that have unquestionably advanced modern life.

If you think going to work is a problem, then quit your job and see what problems that brings! We cannot avoid problems, but when we embrace the opportunities problems bring, we grow, we prosper and, lo and behold, our self-esteem escalates! Because of mountains, we learn to climb.

Problem Solving

Make your problems an opportunity to develop, strengthen, and hone genius, and you will prosper.

Go To The Roar!

As lions age, their teeth start to rot and they are no longer effective in killing their prey. Thus, the oldest lions go to one side of the field where their prey are, while the healthy young lions lie in wait at the other end of the field. When the old lions give out a mighty roar, the startled prey run in the opposite direction and right into the teeth of the waiting hunters. Had the prey run directly towards the roaring lions, they would have been safe as the old lions would not have been able to take them down.

Life is like that. While running from our fears may not result in the same danger as the prey on the Serengeti experience, it will limit the scope of what is available to us in our lives. In fact, the more we run from our fears, the more power we give them to control our lives, to "eat us up." But if we "go to the roar," we actually expand possibilities for ourselves.

Whatever you fear, do that next, and immediately you transform from being controlled by the fear to being in control of it. Even if the fear doesn't disappear altogether, its control over you is weakened while your confidence is strengthened.

Start small and work your way up the ladder of success. For instance, if you have a fear of speaking in front of groups, ask to lead the morning huddle for a week. If you have a fear of rejection, invite an acquaintance to lunch. If you have a fear of being alone, go out to lunch by yourself at a restaurant. In other words, do something that *you* generate rather than waiting for something to happen *to* you. Each time you complete an action, congratulate yourself for your courage and commitment to your own growth.

Discover for yourself that when you go to the roar, the lion has no teeth!

Pearls Of the Harbor

I was in Hawaii for the 74th anniversary of the Japanese attack on Pearl Harbor, "a date which will live in infamy" (President Franklin D. Roosevelt). It is amazing to look back and see the total turn-around of events since then. Japan, Germany, and Italy, our sworn enemies during WW II, are long since our allies, and despite the scourges of war that decimated these countries, they are all thriving economies today.

It's a bit of a stretch in my imagination, but this remarkable transformation reminded me of how pearls develop. Pearls are formed inside an oyster or mollusk when an irritant such as a tiny stone or bit of sand gets inside the shell. A lustrous substance called nacre is secreted around the object to protect the soft internal surface of the mollusk and continues to build up, thus producing the pearl. It's amazing how Mother Nature can take a problem and transform it into a treasure.

We can make pearls in our lives if we treat the irritants in our lives with caring and love. Instead of hardening ourselves against the wrongs we perceive, what if we bathe them in love, positive thinking, and empathy? For instance, suppose a difficult patient comes into the office with a scowl on her face, looking prepared to pounce upon the first team member for some perceived infraction. Instead of getting defensive, fighting back, or letting someone else handle it, what if you saw the patient as someone who was hurting and in need of help, treated her with kindness and love, bathing her in the human form of oyster nacre? Perhaps you could convert your nemesis into one of your strongest allies—a pearl of a patient!

Make pearls out of the irritants and enrich life itself!

Problem Solving

From Breakdown to Breakthrough

In his poem "To A Mouse," Robert Burns mused, *The best laid plans of mice and men often go astray* [paraphrased]. In fact, breakdowns are common. Less common is our reacting rationally to them. Our first reaction is often to blurt out our favorite expletive, but then we feel anger or sadness, perhaps guilt and blame. It is normal to react but non-productive to feel guilty or useless.

The first thing to remember is it's not *bad* to have a negative or emotional reaction to a breakdown or a mistake. Accept your initial reaction but try to block feelings of blame, guilt, and shame. Instead, train yourself to quickly ask, "What can I learn from this?" Or, "How can I use this to further my goals?" When I encounter problems or glitches, one of my first thoughts is, "Can this be a good story to use as a learning moment with my clients?"

If you view the breakdown from only a personal point of view, you will likely take a defensive posture, explaining why it happened and why it wasn't your fault. Instead, shift the conversation to find out what system didn't work, or what procedure was insufficient or outdated, or where training fell short. Then you can create a stepping stone to success in the future. In fact, the most useful response is to look first at the *systems* before looking at the people for the source of the problem. Presume that people are doing the best they can with what they know or with the tools they have. When people know better, or have better tools, they do better.

By stepping away from the emotional reaction to a problem, you can turn breakdowns into break-throughs!

Mistakes are great moments for learning.— **Buckminster Fuller**

To Do or To Be Lists

Many people make up "to do" lists for both their work and home lives. These are especially helpful in organizing, prioritizing, and reminding us what has to be done in our busy and hectic lives. But how many people make up "to be" lists?

How you are *being* makes all the difference in how you go about doing the items on your list. For instance, if you are stressed, annoyed, or even angry, you may be able to mask your feelings but your performance will nonetheless be negatively impacted. Should a problem arise in the middle of it, you will handle it very differently than you would if you were in a calm and relaxed state of mind.

We wake up in the morning and get busy preparing for the day. We tend to our hygiene, feed ourselves and family, organize our schedules, communicate with our families to coordinate pick-up and drop-off times, and so on. How about doing something that will make all the "doingness" easier? Make up a "To Be" list:

Be generous

Be kind

Be open to listening to others

Be happy

Be empathetic

Be loving

These are just a few that you can create with your family and your team in the morning huddle before you "hit the road running." It may not ensure that you don't have any problems or conflicts during the day, but it will change the way you experience them and even the way you handle them.

Remember, we are not human doings, we are human *beings!*

The Joy Job

On occasion, I get a question from a team member wanting to know how to deal with negative people at work, including

Problem Solving

the doctor. The situation is usually one in which the person says she comes to work in a positive attitude but then a coworker enters the scene full of negativity and drags everyone else down. *What should I do?* the caller asks.

The answer is simple, yet complex and challenging: Don't let anyone steal your joy! Joy is actually a natural expression of ourselves. When you watch babies and little children, they seem to be wide-eyed and delighted at the simplest things in life. Facebook and Instagram are filled with photos and videos of children showing exuberance towards things adults find mundane and even boring.

Wonder and joy are natural human states of being, and in sad irony, we are taught not to experience them. As children, we were constantly told what we couldn't do, what was silly and what was hard, what things we should fear. These daily "lessons" came not only from our parents but from other authority figures, such as neighbors and teachers, and they were strongly reinforced by the television shows we watched. Then we became adults!

If you are in a situation where your coworker or your boss is negative, inoculate yourself from them by keeping your focus on what is working in your life or the practice, on serving the patients, and on acknowledging the good around you. Focus on creating and spreading joy.

When you work on patients, you wear gloves and a mask to protect yourself from catching and spreading harmful germs. Don't let others' negativity infect you! Before starting work, remind yourself of the many blessings you enjoy—the benefits of your employment, your friends and family who support you, and, more generally, the freedoms you enjoy as a citizen of a democratic country.

The job of joy may be challenging, but the results are far-reaching and rewarding!

The Silver Box

Although I've never been a parent, I have five nieces whom I watched grow up and evolve into wonderful and beautiful adults. Like all children, they all cried when hungry or hurt, were distressed by sadness or disappointment. But on the whole, they were happy kids, as are most children, in my view. Young ones wake up in the morning ready for a new adventure, eager to discover more of their world, and excited about treasures that learning might reveal. They don't know that Monday is a day to drag out of bed or that Friday is a time to celebrate. Indeed, every day is a great day to be alive.

When did we adults begin to lose that sense of excitement and wonder? Luckily, not all is lost in adulthood. Our fondest and most joyful moments get stored in a "silver box," perhaps literally but more likely figuratively. It is wonderful to retain our best memories from childhood, but what happens if the reality of adulthood leaves us in a constant state of disappointment, even despair? Our "silver box" is something to be cherished, but we can't let it rob us of the ability to experience the fullness of our present life.

We also all have a "black box" that stores all the emotional pains we experienced as children. Dwelling on these negative experiences can keep us stuck in the past and dissipates our sense of adventure as adults. We have to keep our cool, realizing that as adults, we continue to add to both our "silver boxes" and "black boxes."

So don't throw your silver or black boxes in the trash! Recognize all your experiences for what they are—life lessons that have brought you to the present moment. Use them to energize yourself for your next adventure!

Nothing is more precious than being in the present moment. Fully alive, fully aware.— **Thich Nhat Hanh**

Final Thoughts

Consulting and speaking was not my first career. In fact, I was a certified audiologist for the first ten years of my professional life. I then joined a national training and development company, and after seven years I wound up working for a practice management company specializing in orthodontic practices. In 1991, I became an independent consultant. Although I have worked in many different industries, orthodontics has continued to be my niche market.

Among the many twists and turns on this road to the present, there has been one common denominator: I want to make a difference. This is not singular to me. It's one of the basic instincts with which we all came into this world. Very fortunately I have received a lot of support and reinforcement, though there have been many times when I could not see if what I was doing mattered. Still, I stayed the course. My mantra has been, "Keep doing the right things and eventually the right things will happen."

Finally, I thank each of you for being a reader, for encouraging me to keep writing, and for allowing me to be a part of your expanding journey in life. You have truly given me a life worth smiling about.

Appendix

As Mahatma Gandhi famously stated, *All good thoughts and ideas mean nothing without action.* So it is with the messages in this book. Whatever inspiration you derive from reading any essay must be backed by actions that can and will change behavior and produce results. My messages are meant to inform, and possibly entertain, but if they are not *enacted*, then I have failed. With that in mind, I offer a few suggestions on how to *activate* the messages so that they can more effectively improve your personal and work lives.

For example, there is a chapter devoted to gratitude. Gratitude is the best antidote to negativity and poor job performance. Unfortunately, life is filled with conditions and situations that can give one a negative outlook—in fact, it is a matter of *focus* that will determine attitude and subsequent actions.

Here is a suggested action to maintain a positive outlook despite circumstances: As people come into work, and before the start of the morning huddle, ask each person to write on a flip chart "What I am grateful for." The rule is there can be no duplications, so if someone has written "Family," then everyone else has to come up with other items. Keep this going for a week! If you have 10 employees, by the end of the week there will be 50 things for which people are grateful. The following week, change the topic to "What I am proud of" or "What/Whom I love."

Another way to encourage a positive outlook: Each day have someone bring in a short story of someone who overcame great odds to succeed in life. Of course, rotate the assignment so that everyone has to bring in a story. These might be of people who were born with disadvantages either social or physical, or people who were struck with tragedy and succeeded anyway, or just ordinary people who

Appendix

achieved extraordinary results. The internet is full of inspiring stories, so the assignment should not be a burden.

When you want to empower leadership in your team, have the meetings led by a different person each week. You decide on the agenda but the guest leader can be creative in how to enliven, inspire, and promote a great attitude for the day. This exercise helps everyone understand not only what it takes to lead but also how to become a better listener and participant in meetings.

Try this to focus on creating better collaborative relationships among your team: Sponsor "paired luncheons," in which people who don't normally work together have lunch in pairs. It is amazing what a person can find out, and possibly admire, about a team member they barely knew. After lunch, gather as a group and share experiences.

If you want to encourage better relationships among your team, set up a "WOW" board in the staff lounge. Anyone can put a Post-It Note on the board to acknowledge someone else for what that person has done to "wow" another team member or a customer. You can also call this board the "Little Things Mean A Lot." The idea is to visually thank a team member for helping out even with the smallest of tasks.

These exercises focus on creating experiences that drive home the lessons. Experiential learning is more lasting and effective than just reading or talking. The idea is to engage people in activities and experiences that focus on positive ideas and actions. I offer these activities only as suggestions—use them as a starting point and then come up with great ways to kick start you day with positivity!

Acknowledgments

None of us achieves any level of success on our own. We stand on the shoulders of those who came before us, allowing us to reach higher than they could. Nobel Laureate Elie Wiesel said it best in a 1992 commencement address:

> *There is divine beauty in learning, just as there is human beauty in tolerance. To learn is to accept the postulate that life did not begin at my birth. Others have been here before me, and I walk in their footsteps. The books I have read were composed by generations of fathers and sons, mothers and daughters, teachers and disciples. I am the sum total of their experiences, their quests. And so are you.*

In a sense, the Messages I have written here are not just mine, but rather the accumulation of knowledge and lessons I have learned from those who came before me. In 1976, I chose to become a student for life, and set out to learn what I could from books, seminars, workshops, retreats, and teachers who opened my eyes to new possibilities. The common thread throughout these lessons was: *I alone am responsible for my experience of life.*

This realization had the profound effect of freeing me from the enslavement of believing life is happening to me. The essential truth is we have little or no control over the circumstances in life—we can't control the weather, for example, but we are responsible for what we *do* about it. As the noted psychologist Carl Jung said, "I am not what happened to me. I am what I choose to become." I have not always liked the circumstances I have faced, but "liking" is not part of the equation for success and freedom.

My parents, Marie and Paul Garbo, used every tool available to them to provide their children with the opportunities for success. It wasn't until I became a young

Acknowledgments

adult that I recognized they did the best they could with what that had to work with. I am forever grateful for the values of integrity, gratitude, and a belief in God they instilled in me and my four siblings, which proved to be the life lines that pulled me through unsettling times in my life.

My siblings and I grew up believing *blood is thicker than water,* and that has been another safety net for me. We have all "been there" for each other when the chips were down; and even more importantly, we have celebrated life together with great laughter, and a sense of humor we inherited from my mother.

In particular, I have to spotlight my sister Irene Garbo. She has been my editor extraordinaire for every piece I've written, whether for my newsletter or for various publications. She has been ruthless in making sure my messages reflected a commitment to excellence. She has also been my CEO (Chief Encouraging Officer), helping me to meet publishing deadlines as well as pushing me through the writer's block that I encountered from time to time.

Paul Zuelke and Keith McLachlan were readers of my manuscript, and I am indebted to them for their insightful feedback. They came through for me as I knew they would! Thanks also to my book editor, David K. Dodd. He took the 'daunting' out of the process of transforming my idea into a reality and was incredibly easy to work with. My initial concern was that someone who didn't know me would edit and change my voice, but instead he amplified it. I appreciate his wisdom, tact, patience, and guidance in bringing my book into existence.

Finally, I am forever grateful for the many colleagues, friends, and associates who have wanted to hear what I have to say and who have supported me for many years. They have been selfless in sharing their audiences and clients, thus helping me expand my platform. My raison d'être has always been to have a positive impact on the quality of life of as many people as I can reach. I am grateful for all who have granted me the privilege of participating in their life's journey.

About the Author

Joan Garbo has been called a "premier change agent." Over the past forty years, Joan has led more than 2500 seminars on topics such as effective communication skills, self-expression, customer service, team-building and other related topics that enable individuals to experience life more fully and accomplish their goals. Her high energy level, sense of humor, and enthusiasm inspire people to action, giving them a renewed sense of purpose and the resources for self-motivation.

Joan has a Master's degree from the University of Virginia. She spent the first ten years of her career as a certified audiologist in New York City and Long Island hospitals where she increased patient caseload by 100% as a result of her commitment to excellence in patient relations. Joan changed careers in 1978 and became a professional speaker and consultant in new communication technologies. For the past thirty-five years, she has specialized in consulting and training orthodontists and their teams in enhancing their communication and relationship skills and turning their patients into a volunteer sales force.

Joan is a nationally known speaker, addressing such prestigious groups as the American Association of Orthodontists and its constituent associations, various state dental and orthodontic societies, the Tweed Study Group, the Gorman Institute, Ortho2 Users meetings, and Carestream Dental User Meetings for orthodontists, dentists and oral surgeons.

The September 1993 issue of the Houston-based magazine DBA said it best:

"Occasionally life may present us with individuals who possess such a refreshing perspective and tremendous level of

enthusiasm that we are somehow different for having experienced them. Joan Garbo is just such a person.

Monday Morning Messages is Joan's first book. Additional copies can be purchased at Amazon.com or BarnesandNoble.com, and autographed copies are available through her website.

Website: **JoanGarbo.com**

CPSIA information can be obtained
at www.ICGtesting.com
Printed in the USA
JSHW042357011222
34009JS00002B/11